The Wisdom of Dolphins

by Susan Yoder and Major Benton

Sourcebooks, Inc.®
Naperville, IL

This publication is designed to provide accurate and authoritative information in regard to the subject matter covered. It is sold with the understanding that the publisher is not engaged in rendering legal, accounting, or other professional service. If legal advice or other expert assistance is required, the services of a competent professional person should be sought.—*From a Declaration of Principles Jointly Adopted by a Committee of the American Bar Association and a Committee of Publishers and Associations*

Published by Sourcebooks, Inc.
P.O. Box 4410
Naperville, IL 60567-4410
(630) 961-3900 Fax: (630) 961-2168

Library of Congress Cataloging-in-Publication
Yoder, Susan
    The wisdom of dolphins / by Susan Yoder and Major Benton.
        p. cm.
    ISBN 1-57071-461-4 (alk. paper)
    1. Dolphins—Psychology. 2. Human-animal relationships.
I. Benton, Major II. Title
QL737.c432Y64 1999
599.53' 15—dc21   99-30567
                                                                              CIP

Printed and bound in the United States of America
BG 10 9 8 7 6 5 4 3 2 1

TABLE OF CONTENTS

DEDICATION

This book is dedicated to the gray-faced ones.

"And still I break up through the skin of awareness a thousand times a day,
as dolphins burst through seas, and dive again, and rise, and dive."

Annie Dillard, *An American Childhood*

ACKNOWLEDGMENTS

We wish to thank our families, and all our friends and colleagues in the dolphin community, for their help and encouragement.

PREFACE

FOR A LONG TIME, the sea was considered unfathomable, a vast and silent mystery. But it is silent only when you gaze upon it from a distance. If you enter the sea and listen, you can hear many ancient voices, mysterious and beautiful.

Some of those voices belong to dolphins. Humankind's attitudes toward dolphins have changed as our own societies have evolved, and are to some extent a reflection of the evolution of our relationship to non-human animals. Our fascination with marine mammals began long ago. Dolphins have been depicted in pottery and painting, song, and story. Myths from ancient times tell us something about what dolphins were doing back then, and how people were relating to them. And yet we still understand so little about mammals that live in the sea.

Up until as recently as forty or fifty years ago, dolphins were considered fish by many non-scientists—unusual in that they seemed curious and friendly toward people. We find their apparent interest in us intriguing.

From Vickie Shufer, Naturalist, Virginia Beach, Virginia:

While swimming along the shore with a friend, I began whistling and calling to the dolphins, saying, 'Come on dolphins, come play with me.' I was standing in waist-deep water at the time and scanning the horizon for any signs of them, when suddenly right in front of me was a whole pod of dolphins swimming right toward me! They looked huge and I screamed. As they swam around me, they were so close I could almost reach out and touch them. Afterward, my friend and I laughed, remembering how as little girls we would try to get little boys' attention and when we succeeded would scream and take off running.

Because we have only just scratched the surface when it comes to understanding them, dolphins hold great fascination for us, and are the subject of many dreams and imaginings. It can be telling to look at the ways in which people personify other members of the animal kingdom. Some judge dolphins' intelligence to be less than that of a dog; others place them far above us. One person may see dolphins as gentle and sweet, another may see dolphins as awesome and godlike.

Our experiences in the dolphin community have shown us that most people who study and work with dolphins believe it to be most fruitful and appropriate to develop a true understanding of their ways, to appreciate the incredible abilities of mammals adapted to live in the sea—a vastly different world within our world—creatures of skill and intelligence, yet in harmony with their environment in ways we have long forgotten. Another level of wisdom is born from striving to absorb the truth of something, whether that something is a person, an animal, a tree, or a rock. The trick, of course, is to separate "truth" from "imagining."

Joy Hampp was hired in 1985 by the newly organized Dolphin Research Center on Grassy Key, Florida, to create Dolphinlab, their core education program. She soon came to a realization that became the new program's driving force: "I arrived holding certain preconceived notions about dolphins that were quickly dispelled with the privilege of meeting and getting to know them in person. What I discovered is that the reality of dolphins is far more intriguing than the fantasy ever was."

What sort of animal is a dolphin? Dolphins are cetaceans, the order of marine mammals that also includes whales and porpoises. Oceanic dolphins are of the family *Delphinidae*; other toothed whale families are the porpoises and the critically endangered river dolphins, as well as beaked whales, sperm whales, narwhal, and white whales.

There are more than thirty species of oceanic dolphin, most of which are largely mysterious. Many species live out in the deep open sea and, unless they strand, we only catch glimpses of these elusive dolphins. We are most familiar with the bottlenose dolphin (*Tursiops truncatus*), a robust, gray dolphin that often inhabits coastal waters.

This species has proven to be not only approachable, but even interested in people, and is the species most often seen in facilities. Most of the information and stories in this book refer to bottlenose dolphins.

Both bottlenose and Atlantic spotted dolphins (*Stenella frontalis*), also referred to in this book, have been the subject of long-term research that is allowing us to form a picture of what their lives are like. Spotted dolphins are slender, agile dolphins that also seem to be curious about humans and tolerant of our interest in them.

People learn from personal stories and direct experiences, as well as from scientific research. We know personally and through observation the positive effects that can result from being around dolphins. We have many stories from our own experiences, and many confirmed stories from others in the marine mammal community. We've watched members of the general public who come away from guided tours of facilities with a renewed interest in conservation of the marine environment. We've participated in and observed research being done with both wild and captive dolphin populations, and had personal experiences that changed our lives. We've taught programs involving dolphins interacting with people of all ages, and we've seen the results of therapy programs based on dolphin-human interactions that defy sober explanation. Dolphins can be a catalyst for people to experience living in the moment, opening of the heart, laughter, healing, and acceptance.

We're going to convey what we've experienced with examples from personal experiences with wild dolphins in the Bahamas and along the Florida and Virginia coasts, and the dolphin-human interactions that took place at the two Florida Keys facilities where we worked and were privileged to get to know individual dolphins on a day-to-day basis: the Dolphin Research Center on Grassy Key, and the Chicago Zoological Society's Dolphin Connection at Hawk's Cay Resort on Duck Key.

We see this book as an opportunity to share with others what we've been so fortunate to learn ourselves. We hope to convey some of the inspiration that springs from being around dolphins, as well as provide insights we have gleaned from contemplation of the characteristics of dolphins, insofar as they are now known. We include some simple reflections on how dolphin wisdom can be applied in your own life.

We write about dolphins because we have had powerful experiences with them, but we want to point out that dolphins are just one example of the inspiration to be found if you're tuned in to who and what is around you, and within you. The same clarity and connectedness can be felt in many experiences, in the laughter of a child as well as the hum of a swarm of bees. We also want to point out that, while dolphins have become symbols of a kaleidoscope of meaning to different people, the reality of a dolphin is ultimately known, we suspect, only to dolphins themselves.

We've been influenced by the thinking of such people as whale researcher Dr. Roger Payne, who points out that, although marine mammals have large and complex brains and have been on the planet for far longer than we, they show no signs of threatening their own destruction: "They haven't reproduced themselves into oblivion, they haven't destroyed the resources they depend upon, they haven't generated a hole in the ozone layer, or changed the atmosphere so that the earth might end up with a run-away greenhouse effect." In that sense, perhaps there is much we can learn from dolphins.

We don't understand everything the dolphins are saying, but we have begun to listen.

Introduction

CONNECTING

From Susie's Journal, March, 1994:

I'M LYING WITH EYES CLOSED on a floating dock, absorbing the sounds made by the water all around me: lapping around the mangrove roots at the shore, sucking and splashing under the little wooden dock beneath me. The dock is hard and the edges of the uneven boards press into my back. Sometimes the dolphins swim under the dock, rocking me gently. They are in their element, and I in mine, separated by a few wooden boards and millions of years of evolution. Periodically, the dolphins living in this back pool surface to breathe. I try to mimic their breathing with a forceful exhalation and quick inhalation that sounds like: "Te-Puuhh-Kiihh. Te-Puuhh-Kiihh."

It's a quiet time of day at the Dolphin Research Center, between late after-noon and early evening—my favorite time. No other people out here, just me and the critters. The gulls, the egrets, the herons, the fish, the dolphins. Lying here, so close to the water, in the presence of dolphins, I feel a connection with my own inner being, and with all beings—with whatever it is that we have in common in this world.

Toward the end of the age of dinosaurs, another kind of life on Earth began to play the survival game with great success—the mammal. Many mammals thrived on land, but apparently at least one mammal, living close to the sea and finding it a good food source, played around at life as an aquatic mammal. Being a mammal in the sea pre-sented certain awkward challenges, and so began a long process of adaptation.

Meanwhile, back on land, what were to become humans appeared—primates, with clever hands featuring opposable thumbs. Our ancestors began to walk erect, conquered the requirements of survival, and, as time passed, our brains grew larger and ever more complex. We developed speech, written language, religion, organized war, reason, politics, science, and the Dow Jones Industrial Average, not necessarily in that order.

It took us until about the 16th century to realize that our brains apparently served as the mechanism for our thoughts, and had something to do with how we were different from other animals. By this time, we were fairly well along the path of mind—using our brains to develop philosophy, art, and music. The aquatic mammals had continued to refine into extremely successful animals with large brains, not identical to ours, but comparable in size and complexity.

Dolphins' brains differ in structure from ours, and we don't know much about

Marine mammals meet land mammal—trainer Kathy Roberts connects at the Dolphin Research Center.

how they think, but there is little doubt that their cognitive abilities are well developed. We look at them and marvel that they can have such complex minds, and yet apparently not experience the separation we feel from the natural world. Unlike the human race, they seem so harmonious, so attuned to each other and their environment, as if retaining some inherent wisdom we have lost.

From Teresa Winter, author and licensed therapist in Saco, Maine:

Dolphins show us our connectedness, something we need to get back in touch with if we are to survive, just like our intuition. It's all the same. We are them and they are us.

Awakening a Reverence for Life

We sense elemental truths in nature that defy our comprehension. As our civilizations have grown and we have progressed along the paths of mind and spirit, humans have looked to nature for grounding, for inspiration, for clues to who we are. Much of this endeavor is fairly abstract or involves a great deal of projection—we put much of ourselves into our contemplation of the sunset, the mountain, the bird. But as we contemplated dolphins, there was the added dimension of encountering a mind that seemed to comprehend us, and eyes that viewed us with recognition.

From Paula Tiller, Conservation Officer, Wiltshire, England:

A dolphin-watching trip on board a sailing catamaran in the waters of the Atlantic Ocean off Key West had been recommended to me. When we encountered a group of dolphins, I donned mask and snorkel and slipped into the warm water, hopeful of catching a glimpse of a dolphin. The captain had fashioned "aquaplane" boards out of plywood which allowed you to be towed behind the boat while it cruised along at a gentle speed. Tilting the board downward enabled me to fully submerge. A slight incline on the board brought me to the surface, allowing me to clear my snorkel with a sharp exhalation and replenish my lungs with air. Moving along in this way, consciously controlling my breathing, gave me an idea of how it might be as a dolphin coming to the surface and consciously clearing its airway to take in more life-sustaining air.

Contemplating this, I was distracted by a dark shape at my side and my body tingled as I picked up the rapid-fire clicks of echolocation. A glance to my right was rewarded with a view of a large bottlenose dolphin swimming alongside me, no further than six or seven feet away. This beautiful wild creature, graceful and confident in its element, held my gaze. We continued alongside one another for what seemed like several minutes but was probably a matter of seconds.

I do not know what was going on behind the dolphin's steady and commanding brown-eyed gaze, but it moved me deeply. If I shut my eyes, I can clearly recapture that eye-to-eye contact. Once again I can feel the serene calm mixed with elation that washed over me at that time. It was a profound and cherished moment and one which I feel very privileged to have experienced.

Dolphins have an astounding ability to strike a spark that opens us to a deeper reverence for life. It's easy to take for granted what is familiar; to not really see what is right in front of us; to fail to appreciate and respect other life forms. People sometimes forget that we humans are, in fact, part of the natural world. Yet, without a reverence for all life, our individual lives lack richness and meaning.

Native American traditions are full of a sense of reverence for life based on an appreciation of and familiarity with the world in which they live; and a recognition of the unique qualities of each life form. They honor the animals and plants upon which they depend for survival, using the words, "Mitakuye oyasin," meaning we are all related; we are all connected.

Experiences of deep connection with other people can be most powerful, but are sometimes not easily accessible—so often we take each other for granted. The beauty of being around dolphins is that they make it easy—they pull you out of yourself with their energy and spontaneity; they grab your attention, and hold it because of their responsiveness. It's a dynamic interaction eliciting your complete involvement.

What meaning do interactions with dolphins have for people? How do participants in those interactions (including us) describe them? Again and again, we hear about the dolphins' sense of fun and playfulness, their sensuousness, about how uninhibited and spontaneous they are. In trying to verbalize their feelings about being with dolphins, people use words like unconditional love and acceptance, privilege, joy, harmony, and connectedness.

Frame of Reference

It is a quality of our humanity that we seek ourselves in everything around us. We see faces in the clouds, in the rocks, in the trees. We see ourselves in the animal kingdom. It may be anthropocentric to see ourselves everywhere, but it's also an attempt to identify with the patterns repeated over and over in our world, and to understand how we fit in. We are curious animals.

Alike yet different. A spotted dolphin connects with a swimmer in a rare moment.

It is time for humankind to broaden our perspective and allow that dolphins are not above us; they are not beneath us; they are fellow travelers in space and time, sharing our planet Earth. Perhaps we can best connect with them not by looking for ways in which dolphins are like us, but by moving the center point of our inquiry outside ourselves; by considering what kind of beings they are and how we may relate to them not on our terms, but theirs.

From Cori Trudeau, Interpretive Naturalist at the Minnesota Zoo and former dolphin trainer:

The times I treasure most from my years as a dolphin trainer were never during the training session but the times that occurred spontaneously when I was just hanging out with them. I am frustrated by the false image people often have of dolphins. Seeing them as "humanlike" seems to make them more appealing to people. It also keeps people from learning what they are really like. What I found is that dolphins do not need our help improving their image. I like to think of them just as they are.

People feel a powerful emotional connection to dolphins. The difficulty seems to be in how we interpret that connection. One of a dolphin's most impressive intellectual powers is the ability to seemingly go outside its own frame of reference to understand and operate within ours. Can we do the same? Is it possible for people to form an understanding of others beyond the subjective character of their own experience?

In an essay titled "What Is It Like to be a Bat?", Thomas Nagel describes the difficulty of knowing what it is like to be a creature very different from ourselves.

> "…in contemplating the bats we are in much the same position that intelligent bats or Martians would occupy if they tried to form a conception of what it was like to be us. The structure of their own minds might make it impossible for them to succeed…"

If we have to be human to fully understand what it means to be human, can we hope to understand what it means to be a dolphin? How can we hope to connect? Dr. Tom White of Loyola Marymount College, in "Speculations About the Nature of Nonhuman Consciousness, Or, What Is It Like to be a Dolphin?", uses Nagel's essay on understanding non-humans as a point of departure for his discussion of understanding the true nature of dolphins, which he approaches with more optimism. In his view, "Humans and dolphins…are both intelligent mammals. And I believe that this fact makes it more likely…for us to come to at least a basic understanding of dolphins…"

Dr. White goes on to suggest that exploring the ways in which the experience of being a dolphin differs from the experience of being human—physiological differences, differences in physical environment, the imperatives of surviving in the ocean that have led to different forms of communication and social structure—will "let humans begin to understand not only, to adopt Nagel's phrase, 'what it is like to be a dolphin,' but also to recognize an appropriate moral standard for human/dolphin interaction."

Breaking Down Barriers

What about understanding each other? Surely we would benefit as a society and a species by applying ourselves to the problems of comprehending the subjective experience of the people with whom we interact—trying to look at things from their point of view. Perhaps some of the same strategies can be used as are suggested for understanding non-human species, i.e., considering the physical environment which has shaped each person, the differences between their environment and your own, the experiences that are central to their existence, and the circumstances in which they can thrive.

In relating to other living beings, both human and non-human, it is useful to consider both how we are alike and how we are different. In childhood, we learn early to compare ourselves to others. We are satisfied with similarities, and awed by differences. Children are keen observers of "same" and "different;" they also have the ability to absorb what initially seems a difference into their own frame of reference; thus, left to their own devices, two young children of different races are at first fascinated by differences in skin color, shape of facial features, texture of hair, and then quickly seem to focus on the fact that they are essentially alike. They move on to the more important business of play, and of getting to know each other.

As adults, and even older children, this natural acknowledgment and acceptance of differences is buried in layer upon layer of learned behavior, societal and family prejudices, and fear. But we have the ability to connect, to look beyond our narrowed scope of mind, and reconnect with the essence of another being. We can consciously apply mind, heart, and spirit, first to recognizing the barriers that separate us, and then to breaking them down.

Because we are not dolphins, we can't expect to get inside and know them as we know ourselves. Everything is interpreted through the lens of our own selves, our intellects, our emotions, our senses, our experiences. Dolphins are required to obey the laws of dolphin nature just as humans obey the laws of human nature. We have both intriguing similarities and vast differences. But because we humans are part of life on this planet, and we have certain physical and biological commonalities with other life forms, it is not unreasonable to expect that the energy behind our lives is of the same stuff. We are all connected.

Part One   C O M M U N I T Y

Dolphins are sociable animals. Like wolves, apes, elephants, and people, dolphins live together as unified individuals, linked by common experiences and concerns. Groups of dolphins are commonly called pods. It is doubtful we can arrive at any worthwhile understanding of dolphins without considering them in the context of what we've seen of their social interactions.

Each chapter in this section explores an aspect of what it means to be part of a dolphin community. Basic to living in a group is the ability for individuals to *communicate* with each other—and how dolphins communicate with each other, and with humans, is a fascinating realm of study.

What are the ties that bind members of a dolphin pod? Certain kinds of *relationships* are notable in dolphin society, and they may not be what you would expect.

Cooperation certainly takes place at a sophisticated level, as dolphins act together to hunt for food, protect their pod from predators, support weaker members, and care for their young.

Finally, it is important to realize that a cooperative society doesn't preclude uniqueness; it is, in fact, enhanced by it. Just as each person has character traits that distinguish him or her as a unique *individual*, each dolphin has personality differences, and responds uniquely to its environment.

COMMUNICATION

THE USE OF LANGUAGE was long considered something that set the human race apart from the rest of the animal kingdom. As we have begun to recognize and investigate the capabilities of other intelligent mammals, we, perhaps naturally, have looked for signs that we can hope to "talk with the animals."

Although the physiological equipment involved in a dolphin's communication is far different from ours, there are some similarities, i.e., we both use sound and body language. But in spite of numerous studies designed to identify a dolphin "language" in which certain sounds represent objects or actions, little is known about how dol-

Above: Omega, part of the Dolphin Research Center family of dolphins, works her magic in a Dolphin/ Child therapy session.

phins communicate. We are still a long way from understanding what their sounds might mean.

Attempting to decipher a mode of communication very different from our own can be both humbling and enlightening. Heidi Lerner, Special Educator aboard the research vessel *Stenella*, puts into words some of the mystery of the underwater world she has experienced:

Sea of Translucence

Tints and shades array themselves into colors.

Blended yet discrete—such a display sedates the mind's torrid currents.

Water, mayim, agua, nuk, vasser,

Tinted in aquamarine-, deep-, dark-, storm-, navy-, cerulean-blue.

And this is home for the sea creatures.

*The rooftop only hints at the great variety of inhabitants in its waters
   and on the ocean floor.*

Purity and elegance dwell inside.

Our imperfect minds glimpse the fathomless excellence of nature's way.

Such grace is savored in interspecies communication.

Touched upon only briefly, yet held onto forever.

Dolphins have access to a rich repertoire of signals to communicate what is necessary in their everyday lives. Dolphins live primarily in an acoustic world, but they are also visually oriented, and use their acute senses of touch and perhaps even taste to weave the tapestry of meaning that bonds their society.

There's no evidence that dolphins convey complicated abstractions to each other, or have a syntactical language like humans, in which we make sounds into words to symbolize specific things, and how the words are combined changes the meaning. Syntax is what tells us a venetian blind is not a blind Venetian. Humans are the animal specialized for this type of language—our vocabulary and use of syntax allows us to communicate not only facts, but abstract thought. Dolphin communication may have more to do with immediate situations, relationships, and emotions.

Dolphin Sounds

Although we are still a long way from understanding what dolphin sounds might mean, marine mammal scientists have, with ingenuity and vast patience, been able to fit together a few pieces of the puzzle. For instance, each dolphin calf develops a "signature whistle"—unique to that dolphin—which researchers believe identifies it to others in the group. They imitate each other's signature whistles, apparently as a way of making contact. Studies also indicate that a dolphin modifies its signature whistle in response to a given situation, giving the sound additional depth of meaning. A dolphin's signature whistle is the only whistle for which researchers have been able to theorize a possible meaning. A dolphin makes a great many others sounds which simply do not fit any patterns of communication we recognize, though research continues.

The wordless communication of dolphins is reminiscent of the wordless language of music. Clearly, musical tones—pitch, volume, rhythm, the order in which notes are arranged, harmony—can convey a wealth of meaning, form pictures in the mind, give rise to concepts and ideas, and can certainly convey emotion and mood. Indeed, hearing music can instantly change a person's mood. Perhaps dolphins use rhythmic patterns as a subtle but powerful element in their communication.

Although wild dolphins rarely vocalize above the water, when around people, dolphins at facilities will poke their heads above the surface and "talk up a storm"— squealing, clicking, and screeching to attract attention. One staff member at the Dolphin Research Center found herself being mimicked by a dolphin when she laughed. Hers was a distinctive "eh-eh-eh-eh-eh" kind of laugh, and she started noticing that Delphi, a highly inventive adult male dolphin, was laughing back at her in the same voice!

Of course, there's a limit to how much dolphins can sound like us. Whereas we use our mouths to speak, breathe, and eat, dolphins have two separate systems—a blowhole for breathing, and a mouth for eating. There is no connection between the two systems. Dolphins have no vocal cords. They are incapable of using lips, mouth, or tongue to form words as we do when we speak. There is no air passing through a dolphin's throat.

All of a dolphin's underwater "vocalizations"—whistles, clicks, and various barks and chirps termed "burst-pulse" sounds—come from structures in the blowhole area at the top of its head. The blowhole, which is closed by a muscular flap when relaxed, opens into the nasal passage which goes to the dolphin's lungs. A dolphin can manipulate the air sacs beneath its blowhole, and possibly other structures, to produce a variety of sounds underwater which do not require any release of air. Above-water sounds are made using the blowhole flap, like letting air out of a balloon.

The Role of Echolocation

Although they may lack words, dolphins are remarkable, acoustic animals: they can process sound ten times faster than humans and can hear pitches ten times higher. They possess an extremely sophisticated echolocation system, a biological "sonar," similar to that of bats. Dolphins don't echolocate all the time, but they can use this important sense to navigate in murky water, to hunt for fish, and to explore.

When a dolphin echolocates, clicks are generated in the blowhole area and sent out through a waxy "lens" in the forehead called the melon. These sound waves bounce off objects in the dolphin's path and return as echoes. We don't know exactly how this "looks" to the dolphin, but echolocation is often compared to ultrasound and may present them with three-dimensional images.

When you are underwater with dolphins, they often "buzz" you with their echolocation, moving their heads in small side-to-side movements, and focusing on areas of your body that interest them. They are adept at pinpointing any foreign substance in a person's body, such as metal plates or pins, and will even focus on places where broken bones have healed.

Echolocation allows dolphins to read air spaces, densities, and movements, even within the body. We can only speculate on how it may affect communication among themselves. Could you tell something about your friend's emotional state by getting a read on her heartbeat, for instance? When a person lies, there are distinct physiological changes—what if we lived in a society where it was impossible to practice deceit?

During one swim encounter at the Dolphin Research Center, the dolphins kept echolocating on a woman's abdomen, prompting the trainers to ask her if she had had any surgery that might have required metal being left in her body. There was nothing she could imagine that would cause them to focus on her. When a trainer asked if she might be pregnant, she said no. A little over two weeks later, the same woman called the Dolphin Research Center to report that, upon arriving home from her vacation in the Keys, she had discovered that she was, in fact, pregnant!

The trainers felt that the dolphins were able to pick up the second heartbeat, or recognize the fluid sac containing the fetus. When a dolphin is pregnant, others in her pool will echolocate on her abdomen, performing their own "ultrasounds."

Language of the Body

Although sound plays a role in communication between dolphins, body language and posturing are the social glue which bonds dolphin society. We have only scratched the surface when it comes to understanding what it all means, but observation of wild pods as well as dolphins in human care makes it apparent that dolphins express themselves through jumps, mimicry, caresses, postures, and rhythm. Leaps and spins, with the resulting splashes, may serve as directional markers defining the dimensions of a wild pod and help keep the group in sync. Some patterns of behavior, such as periods of caressing, seem to be a way of reinforcing trust and checking in with pod members.

Studies have shown that in conversation, only a small percentage of communication among people is verbal: most of our meaning is conveyed through body language and tone of voice—just as a dolphin can alter its signature whistle to convey different meaning. Try saying this sentence over and over, each time stressing a different word: "I think I like her." Your posture, your facial expressions, your gestures, and your tone of voice are at least as important as your words.

Choosing Your Words

Perhaps we expect too much from words. Humans have developed extremely complex languages, yet constantly have trouble communicating! Native Americans put a high premium on silence, and were bemused by the chattiness of Europeans.

They believed the silent, contemplative man was to be trusted, while those who talked too readily were not to be taken seriously. As Chief Joseph of the Nez Perce said, "The white man has more words to tell you how things look to him, but it does not require many words to speak the truth."

When we've been close to dolphins, words seem foreign to the nature of the experience. And yet, ultimately, we feel an urgency to put it into words, as Major does in this excerpt from the journal of his experiences on a research vessel studying spotted dolphins in the Bahamas:

> *For perhaps an hour I was alone with thirteen dolphins. How can I tell the story? Where are the words? Why couldn't I talk to anyone afterwards or answer their questions of what it was like?*
>
> *I was wonderfully lost in another world. I had absolutely no thought of anything other than what was occurring at the moment. The "message" didn't seem to be some attempt at understanding the dolphin language or communication system, but about humans living together more productively and peacefully—the "we are all connected" concept.*
>
> *Constant eye-to-eye contact always said more than any communicating I could have dreamed of by the ordinary standards of sound. The rubs I was given by the sides of their bodies, dorsals, and pecs were only returned by my accepting them and not pulling away. I never felt any need to physically reach out to*

them or pursue them. They accepted me on their terms; I accepted them on theirs as well.

The message was not one of how we can interact with dolphins and learn to communicate with them (for they "talked" to me in their language and I to them in mine), but how we humans can communicate better with our own kind. Yes, there will be misunderstandings, cliques, hierarchies, love, joy, political posturings, games, entanglements to work through, but we can be so much more successful at life and get done what absolutely must get done by being more open and receptive, more giving, more trusting, and more unconditional in everything we do.

Dolphins somehow communicate so well without words that even we, a very different species, can get the message. Try using the same gentle focus to connect with those around you. First, be sure you know what you wish to communicate (having your message clear in your own mind before you speak is half the battle). Relax and center yourself, and notice everything you can about those to whom you're speaking. Then look them in the eyes, and speak simply.

The flip side of communication is to listen well. Allow others to finish speaking before offering a reply. Sometimes no reply is needed beyond simple acknowledgment; the listening validates the speaker. A dolphin, when it chooses to give a human being its full attention, can pick up on the most subtle non-verbal signals, which the human often doesn't realize he or she is giving out. Listening requires more than hearing—it requires engaging your heart, mind, and other senses, as well as your ears. Try giving people your full attention when they talk to you, listening with your whole body, and looking beyond the words.

RELATIONSHIPS

WHILE MUCH OF bottlenose dolphin society remains a mystery to us, scientific observers over the past fifty years have been piecing together the fragments of dolphin life they have seen, and have identified at least some general relationships. Although dolphins tend to move around and travel with different sub-groupings, they often form strong individual bonds. The strongest is the bond between mother and calf, as is true in many species. A dolphin is not loyal to a single mate, but groups of females, as well as pairs of males, may form strong bonds and travel together for years.

Above: Aphrodite and her son A.J. at the Dolphin Research Center.

Dolphin societies are often described as fluid or dynamic, meaning that group-ings of individuals within a pod will shift and change. Mothers and calves seem to form the basic family unit, and travel in the largest groups that include other adult females that help with child care and foraging.

Caring for the Young

In the first few months of its life, a dolphin calf spends most of its time with its mother, and one other adult female, who may have acted as "midwife" and who now swims with the mother and calf. Depending on circumstances and the personalities involved, this relationship loosens up over time, although the female assistant will resume her protective role in a threatening situation.

As calves grow past the age of nursing (after about two years) and become increasingly able to find food, they start to split off from the maternity pods and form juvenile pods of young males and females where they can exercise their indepen-dence and practice hunting and social skills. These groups of youngsters usually stay fairly close to the larger maternity group and can rejoin it in times of danger or for help in finding food.

Male Bonding

Researchers believe that as a male bottlenose dolphin grows into sexual maturity, at about ten to twelve years of age, he will gradually spend less time with the maternity or juvenile groupings, and form bonds with other adult males. These males apparently are not welcome around the young calves—they play too roughly. So they travel in small groups or pairs, and will take advantage of mating opportunities as groups come together. When the adult males mix with females, mothers or babysitters supervise the little ones.

Much as we would like to think of dolphins as peaceful and non-aggressive, the fact is that aggressive behavior has been observed in various dolphin species in many areas of the world. Males may use force to dominate a female during periods of mating. Even pair-bonded males may fight for mating time with the same females. There is a hierarchy within groups, and the leader may use aggressive behavior to establish his or her position. Dolphins come and go between groups, but within each small group there is apparently a sense of what each dolphin's position is. No doubt this avoids chaos—it's good to know where you stand.

Susan Barco, along with a team from the Virginia Marine Science Museum, has been studying wild bottlenose dolphins along the Virginia coast since 1991. She observes:

> *Aggression is a natural part of any complex animal society and I don't think that's any different for dolphins. It's just that we've always wanted them to be so peaceful. Because they are as attuned to their environment as any animal can be—they swim so easily, they breathe so easily, and they look so perfect in their environment—we want that to project to their entire lives.*

Aggression is certainly a part of their lives, just like predation is a part of their lives. There's a wide range of emotions that they display, if you say that they have emotions. There's the very caring caress of a mother to her calf, but then there's also a much more aggressive bite from a dominant male to a less dominant male, or a dominant male to a calf that gets in the way when the male tries to mate with its mother.

Dolphins are very much in balance with nature—something that most of us are not. An animal society that takes aggression too far is a society that's not going to survive, because they're going to end up killing each other, kind of like humans do.

Dolphin Comrades

Bottlenose dolphins in the wild are known to associate with other species, such as pilot whales, spotted dolphins, Risso's dolphins, rough-toothed dolphins, and humpback whales. Dolphins in facilities also socialize with many different species. At the Dolphin Research Center, dolphins sometimes spend free time with the resident sea lion family—they even cooperate during training sessions. While dolphins may socialize with many different individuals, they have preferences and spend most of their time with the animals with whom they seem to feel most comfortable.

Delphi and Kibby are two adult male dolphins who have lived together for many years at the Dolphin Research Center. While they take full advantage of mating opportunities and flirt through the fence with the females in the next pool, Delphi and Kibby are considered inseparable and are a good example of male pair bonding. If one of them is gated into an adjoining pool to take part in research sessions, the other will stay close to the fence and watch his friend's every move. Delphi is the older of the two and appears to be the one in control, with Kibby acting as sidekick. When another male dolphin named Natua lived in the same lagoon, he often was seen by himself; it was Delphi and Kibby who stuck together. These two usually can be seen side by side, either cruising their pool, or as close as possible to the beach, where they seem to enjoy shrieking, clicking, and waving to attract the attention of passing people.

At Chicago Zoological Society's Dolphin Connection, a new dolphin who had been in a facility in California was added to the group. This particular dolphin had once been part of a group that included one of the dolphins already at the Dolphin Connection. Initially, she was put into a lagoon next to the resident dolphins, to allow her to get acclimated before introducing her to the others. The dolphin who had been with her years before faced her through the fencing and the two "talked" incessantly for about thirty minutes. It was obvious to the trainers that these two dolphins instantly recognized each other, and seemed anxious to be together again. If only the trainers could have understood what all the clicks, whistles, and various sounds meant. Did they relay information about what their lives had been like since last parting? Only the dolphins know for sure.

Pilot whales are large, mostly black cetaceans with bulbous heads and very short beaks. Like the large cetaceans we call killer whales, they are members of the dolphin family. Pilot whales are very social animals, sometimes gathering in groups of hundreds or even thousands, and they are known for frequent mass strandings.

From Laura Urian Engleby, Dolphin Research Center Director of Education, 1989-93:

Lumpy, named for a grapefruit-sized bump on her dorsal fin, was one of three pilot whales rescued from a mass stranding in Key West. We had already lost one of the three, and now Lumpy and the other whale, Scarlett, remained together all the time, under the watchful care of our medical team. On this particular day, Lumpy worried me. She just wasn't acting normal; she appeared disoriented. I had a bad, gut feeling that Lumpy was dying. There was no way I could feel the pain she was feeling, but I sensed the life leaving her body. I sat on the dock and watched her for a long time. Tears started to form in my eyes—I felt intensely sad, partly because I didn't want to see her go, and partly because I hated to see her suffer. It's such a helpless feeling when there is nothing you can do to save a whale or dolphin, and you know that you have to let go.

As I watched, Lumpy swam into the mangroves, beaching herself. I ran over to the causeway to push her back out. Scarlett came to her side. Mandy came out to help and we assembled a small group of people to put her in a stretcher. As we held Lumpy, Scarlett began ramming us, trying to push us out of the way, prac-tically getting in the stretcher with Lumpy. It was at that moment that Lumpy took her last breath.

I will never forget how, after Lumpy died, Scarlett raced around their pen in circles a couple of times, vocalizing very loudly. Then she stopped in front of the floating dock, and for hours vocalized non-stop, so loudly I could hear it clearly from the boardwalk. I have never heard such intense vocalizations in my life! It was sad, haunting, and desperate.

Dolphins Bonding with Humans

Natua was the second calf to be born at the facility that was to become the Dolphin Research Center. His mother, Theresa, had a lenient mothering style, and after she gave birth to Natua, Theresa spent most of her time with the other adult dolphins in their pool. Nat soon began to investigate his new human friends, who were delighted to have a chance to interact with a dolphin baby who first came to the dock to see them when he was barely a week old! He never did form particularly strong bonds with the other dolphins, instead becoming a very people-oriented dolphin. As he grew, his extraordinary patience, flexibility, and curiosity were reflected in the strong bonds he formed with people.

The staff was small in those days, and Nat spent most of his time with Mandy Rodriguez, Executive Vice President and co-founder of the Dolphin Research Center.

Mandy is a remarkable dolphin trainer with thirty years' experience. Mandy's approach to training has always been to be "consistently inconsistent." In other words, the dolphins never know what to expect, and stay interested and involved with the training session. With a whole repertoire of lessons ready to be implemented in response to the dolphin's actions, Mandy's sessions stress spontaneity and creativity. He says, "Dolphins and humans function as mirrors, reflecting and affecting each other's actions. Working with marine mammals is very dynamic—everything moves forward quickly."

Nat was fascinated with Mandy and his approach to interaction, and the two formed one of the strongest bonds between human and dolphin that anyone has ever observed. They each invested their time and attention, and were rewarded with a relationship that reflected the best part of themselves, a relationship full of trust, respect, and love.

Mandy with Aphrodite at the Dolphin Research Center.

The Ties That Bind Us

The bond between dolphin mother and calf is as strong as any in nature. Our children remind us of innocence, and the strength of the deepest love. For women, carrying a child and giving birth can bring a sense of fulfillment, put them in touch with their bodies in a new way, and release ancient wisdom they did not know they possessed. For men and women, having children can rearrange priorities, reveal new profundities, and even inspire sacrifice.

Perhaps because they are so vital, our relationships can be problematic. We build barriers and hide behind them. We question who we are and where we stand in relation to those around us. First you must clarify how you want to fit in. What are the strengths you have to contribute? Each dolphin in a pod is different. They balance themselves out, and so do we. Find those who bring out the best in you, and who treat you well. Don't be afraid to open your heart to such people.

What relationships are important in your life? It is the reflections of ourselves in the living mirrors around us that teach us who we are. It is the love of friends and family that give us courage and make our lives beautiful. It is human solidarity that sustains us. Honor your own life, and honor your relationships.

COOPERATION

ANY SUCCESSFUL ANIMAL must have a good strategy for meeting its basic needs. It must eat, and it must reproduce. Mammals are particularly noted for their care-giving behaviors, and dolphins have developed complex systems of social behavior to facilitate finding and catching food, and raising their young. It is, naturally, to their advantage to cooperate with each other.

Depending on the species, dolphins form pods varying in size from a few individuals to thousands. The size of the group seems to depend upon what is supportable by their food supply; in other words, when food is plentiful, a larger group may

Above: Synchronicity—Sisters Merina, Aleta and Santini at the Dolphin Research Center.

have greater success in foraging. If the food supply is patchy, smaller groups will probably have more success.

In general, dolphins that live in shallow coastal waters, such as bottlenose dolphins, form smaller groups than dolphins that live in deep waters farther out in the open sea, such as spinner and spotted dolphins. Bottlenose dolphins form groups and sub-groups numbering from a few individuals to perhaps fifteen to twenty. The pelagic, or open sea, species travel in large groups numbering in the hundreds, which is very useful for finding the schools of fish upon which they feed.

Swimming as a pod is a beautifully synchronized event. When hunting, spinner dolphins spread out in formations that may be miles across, somehow organized to maximize the use of their echolocation, and congregate when part of the group comes across a rich food supply. A group of dolphins will encircle the school of fish, and keep them "penned" in their midst, while individuals take turns going in and feeding.

Another feeding strategy involves forming a line and swimming toward shore to herd schools of fish up onto a shallow bank where they can be picked off. In some places, dolphins chase fish onto mud flats, beaching themselves to feed, then wriggling back into the water.

For generations, dolphins in Brazil have cooperated regularly with local fishermen. When they see the dolphins approach, the fishermen will wade into shallow water with their nets and watch the dolphins carefully. The dolphins herd fish toward the nets, and feed on the confused fish that escape from the fishermen. Both fishermen and dolphins get ample food.

It's hard to know from observing dolphins in facilities how close their behavior is to that of dolphins in the wild. Yet, some of their capabilities come shining through. Just as pods of wild dolphins can travel at high speeds in groups of hundreds with almost miraculous grace and precision, dolphins in facilities perform group behaviors that are a marvel of timing and coordination. Five dolphins can race around a pool, turn together on a dime, and burst from the water in beautiful formation. They are trained to know what they are being asked to do, but the ability and the timing are theirs.

A film crew was at the Dolphin Research Center working with two young female dolphins, Annessa and Aleta. All that separates the dolphin pools from the rest of Florida Bay are large-mesh plastic fences that are designed to keep out the majority of the seagrass and large sharks. The fences were dropped so the cameras could get a nice, clear uninterrupted shot of the open water. Small schooling fish were able to come into the lagoon, which is bordered by a bank of coral rock, and when Anna and Aleta weren't being filmed, they were fishing.

During one break in the filming, as the two dolphins swam about, waiting for activities to resume (they seemed more interested in the cameras than in exploring the ocean outside their pool), we realized they had corralled a school of ballyhoo and were herding the fish up against the coral bank. Not being hungry, they didn't seem interested in eating many fish; the beneficiaries were the herons and gulls that gathered for the feast.

Protecting the Pod

Dolphins have few predators; their greatest dangers in today's world come from people. Aside from us, sharks can be a terrible threat. Sharks probably won't attack a group of healthy dolphins, but will try to pick off the weak, the sick, the old, and the very young. Dolphins will avoid sharks as much as possible, but if attacked, will protect their pod by fighting the shark together. Dolphins can kill a shark by ramming it with their hard snouts, crushing the shark's internal organs.

A dolphin that is sick or old may begin to experience difficulty in getting to the surface to breathe. Pod members may swim with the struggling dolphin, supporting it at the surface so it can move with less effort and breathe more easily. This may be the innate behavior responsible for the many stories of dolphins helping people lost at sea. It seems strange that an animal with such fine powers of discrimination would come to the aid of a struggling human, who certainly looks much different from a struggling dolphin, but the stories are too numerous to discount.

One woman who survived the explosion of a yacht found herself in shark-infested waters. She reported being surrounded and supported by dolphins until she was able to climb out onto a buoy—she had been carried almost two hundred miles from the scene of the accident!

Another such story comes from a pair of senior citizens, experienced naturalists who rented a canoe in Flamingo City to camp for a couple of nights and explore the many islands and waterways on the southern tip of mainland Florida. The trip started out fine, but on the afternoon of their second day, they found themselves further from land than they had anticipated. They had been excitedly paddling alongside a manatee and followed it long enough to get some great photos.

When they turned the canoe around to head back to their campsite, they were shaken into reality by the sight of a heavy rain squall headed their way. Try as they might, they were simply not strong enough to paddle the canoe against the rising winds, and feared they would capsize.

The couple claim they would never have made it safely to shore if a pod of seven dolphins had not appeared on the scene. The dolphins placed themselves on either side of the canoe, just far enough forward and away to allow the couple to paddle while the dolphins broke the water resistance ahead. At one point, the couple felt they actually were being drafted along by the dolphins because their paddles alone could not have propelled them through the water as fast as they felt they were moving.

When the canoe was close enough to shore for the trees to break the strength of the wind blowing against them, the dolphins left as quickly as they had appeared, and the couple reached their campsite safely. No one can convince these two canoeists that dolphins do not have thinking abilities or are not willing to help humans when they can.

Voluntary Medical Behaviors

Dolphins demonstrate an amazing willingness to cooperate with the humans who care for them. An important part of working with dolphins at facilities today is the training of medical procedures. Dolphins learn voluntary behaviors, such as presenting their tail flukes to allow a blood sample to be taken. Blood vessels in the tail flukes are large and easily accessible: the veins are visible as grooves resembling the veins in a leaf. The dolphin learns to allow the trainer to hold its tail flukes in her lap as she presses on a vein with her thumbnail to simulate the procedure. After weeks of training, by the time an actual needle is inserted in the vein to draw blood, the dolphin has become comfortable with the procedure.

Linda Erb, Director of Animal Care & Training at the Dolphin Research Center, with Tursi presenting her tail for blood samples and inspection.

When blood is taken, the dolphin is shown the needle indicating to the dolphin that this is not just practice. The training acclimates them to the procedure, but we could not begin to do this without the dolphins' cooperation. An adult bottlenose dolphin could easily break our legs with its flukes, but instead is careful, and holds still to allow this important work to be done; then waits until the trainer has placed its tail back in the water before flexing its flukes and taking off.

Optimizing Group Potential

How much better could we cooperate with each other if we applied a dolphin's curiosity, flexibility, and persistence to the task? Cooperation requires that we put aside immediate personal concerns and consider the benefits to the community. It's not about proving you are right or have the best idea. It is about respecting our differences, recognizing what each individual has to contribute, and working to optimize the potential of the group.

From the earliest days of civilization, people have lived together in villages or nomadic tribes. These groups provided protection from hostile elements of the environment—from predators to rivals—and made it easier to secure food, whether through hunting, foraging, or agriculture. We learned to share the work, and we learned to diversify. Living in groups provided opportunities for mating, and we figured out ways to avoid counter-productive fighting over mates (well, sometimes). We learned to cooperate.

Our society is a complicated mass of cooperative effort, much of it built-in or automated. You need shelter, protection from cold and danger? You buy a house or rent an apartment. Other members of society, people you probably don't know, have built the structure—architects drew the plans, bankers financed the building, workers laid the bricks, electricians wired the rooms, factory workers assembled the furnishings, and so on—all so you could turn a key, walk through a door, turn on lights, and sit down to rest. You do your part by working at some other endeavor that society deems worthy, so you can pay for your dwelling.

Even primitive societies are specialized to the extent that individuals have different jobs, such as gathering or growing plants, tending or hunting animals, and preparing food. In a complex modern society, we often don't see the people upon whose work we rely, and yet we need each other desperately. We have different skills, we have different work styles, and we express ourselves differently.

The key is first to recognize how people differ in their approaches to a given situation, and then appreciate that these differences are not only acceptable, but can be a source of strength for the community. There are tools designed to assess people's styles of communication and behavior, such as the Myers-Briggs Type Indicator Survey, which reveals built-in preferences in your orientation to life (introversion or extroversion), the way you take in information (physical senses or intuition), how you make decisions (thinking or feeling), and how you deal with the world (judging or perceiving). Identifying strengths and weaknesses in yourself and others—and accepting that we don't all have to have the same approach—not only enhances cooperation and the reaching of goals, but makes for a more pleasant environment.

INDIVIDUALITY

THEY AREN'T MUCH ALIKE: Delphi is meticulous, Kibby is haphazard. Delphi is suave with the lady dolphins, Kibby is boisterous and gawky in comparison. Delphi goes to great pains to figure out what you are asking of him; he seems uncomfortable if he doesn't know the plan, and the training staff is very careful that this dolphin's perfectionism doesn't lead to stress, particularly when he is learning something new. Kibby is much more laid back.

One way that dolphins at the Dolphin Research Center make clear the differences in their personalities is through their painting styles. Many of the dolphins learn to

Above: Kibby painting at the Dolphin Research Center.

hold a paintbrush in their mouths and paint canvases and t-shirts held out over the water within their reach. Some dolphins approach this activity with great enthusiasm; some just aren't interested. Delphi holds a paintbrush carefully in his mouth and marks the canvas with precision; Kibby drops the brush, holds it sideways, dashes away at the canvas, and slops paint and salt water everywhere (usually on you, if you're holding the canvas, and sometimes on himself).

It is obvious to those who work with them that dolphins have distinct, well-developed personalities. Each dolphin has a characteristic way of approaching a task. Dolphins learn in different ways, just as people do. They exhibit definite preferences as to the games they play, what motivates them, and the dolphins and people with whom they interact. They relate to their family and pod members in varying ways. Within a group, each has its niche—perhaps a reflection of the advantages of biodiversity. A diverse population is clearly stronger and more resilient than one in which the individuals resemble each other too closely.

Theresa is one of the grand old ladies of the Dolphin Research Center pod. No one knows exactly how old she is, but she is at least in her thirties, having come to Grassy Key around 1968. The Dolphin Research Center and other colonies include dolphins in their thirties and possibly forties, but early records often are unclear or nonexistent. There are records from studies of wild bottlenose dolphins that show they can live into their fifties—a dolphin can be aged by extracting a tooth, cross-sectioning it, and counting the rings.

Theresa makes people laugh. She is a robust dolphin with double chins, a very pink rostrum (snout), and an unmistakable twinkle in her eye. Trainers trying to do any serious work with Theresa had better have a sense of humor to match hers, because she is just as likely to soak you with her trademark ugly flip (she starts into a flip, then lands flat on her back—big splash!), as to do anything resembling the behavior you just asked for.

Theresa's smiling face and double chins.

Theresa loves to show off another invention of hers that has been dubbed her motorboat impersonation. Trainers guess she picked up the sound from listening to boats going by, but however she came up with it, she began to add a steady "brrrrmm" noise from her blowhole as she sped around the pool. While the other dolphins merely race around the pool to demonstrate their speed and agility, Theresa brings down the house with her speeding motorboat act, tosses her head and looks around at the onlookers to make sure they appreciate her offering.

Another side of Theresa is her nurturing ability: she is a reliable and wise teacher of young dolphins, and she teaches us about lightening up and not taking ourselves too seriously.

Tursi is what one might call a very protective mother, with a possessive mothering style she seems to have learned from her own mother, Little Bit (one of the original inhabitants of the Dolphin Research Center). Tursi kept tight control over her first calf, her son Talon, keeping him close by her side for years. Should little Talon wander off to explore, she quickly rounded him up. She couldn't stand to have him out of her sight, and would stay at the dock during a feeding or training session only if he was right next to her. Tursi kept this up longer than any of the other mothers at DRC. Talon set DRC records by still occasionally nursing when he was three, and Tursi kept a close eye on him until Talon was almost six years old. Trainers were relieved to see that with her second calf, Pax, Tursi seemed much more relaxed.

Then there's Aphro. Aphrodite came to the Dolphin Research Center when it was determined that she required special medical care. She thrived at DRC, and DRC fell in love with her, dubbing her the "porcelain dolphin" for her smooth, silvery gray skin, unmarred by the rake (tooth) marks you usually see resulting from dolphin social activity. Although a relatively petite dolphin, Aphrodite seems to have what it takes to stay on top of the social hierarchy.

From the beginning, Aphro seemed to swim to the beat of a different drummer and quickly developed a reputation as a tremendous tease (Aphro loves to ad lib behaviors, usually the opposite of what the trainer asks). When her son A.J. was born in 1988, Aphro proved to be an extremely lenient mother. Only weeks after delivering A.J., she allowed him to be off by himself exploring. When he was only ten months old, Aphrodite took A.J. over DRC's perimeter fences sometime during the night's high tide, and both were waiting outside the gate in the morning! On his second birthday, A.J.'s little dorsal fin appeared alone outside of the perimeter fences to the trainers' surprise. Obviously, he was developing into an independent young dolphin. If it had been Talon, Tursi would have had a fit. Aphro, on the other hand, seemed unconcerned.

Misty was one of the dolphins who learned to paint t-shirts and canvases by holding a brush in her mouth, and she painted very nicely. She was a dabber—her paintings had many polka dots. But she required a great deal of encouragement and applause—if your appreciation and cheerleading were inadequate, Misty was likely to spit the brush into the water and give you a pained expression, as if to say, "Ho, hum. Is that the best you can do?" Misty's indomitable spirit and challenging ways taught us a great deal about self-confidence, and meeting a dolphin halfway.

Misty was famous for frustrating Dolphinlab students. (Dolphinlab is a week-long education program offered for college credit at the Dolphin Research Center that includes opportunities for the students to get to know the members of the dolphin colony.) A beautiful, athletic adult female with a strong personality, Misty would brook no uncertainty from new trainers or students. She was a great trainer of trainers, requiring accuracy and confidence from them. She was a keen observer, and learned quickly that she could manipulate humans—as a new trainer learned in her second week at the Dolphin Research Center.

Laura was just learning the ropes from DRC's head trainer, Linda Erb. Working with Misty, Linda demonstrated how to hold a hoop out to show the dolphin, then dip it in the water so Misty could go rocketing through—a great game. Laura took the hoop and tried what she had been shown, holding out the hoop, then dipping it into the water. Misty went flying through, hooking the hoop with her dorsal fin and pulling Laura off the dock and into the water. Misty came back to the dock just screaming with delight, eyes twinkling, beside herself with joy. The new trainer hauled herself dripping onto the dock, and with Linda's encouragement, tried again. This time when Misty expertly hooked the hoop, Laura had the presence of mind to let go. When Linda held the hoop, Misty swam smoothly through with perfect grace. It was a month before Misty would swim through the hoop for Laura without trying to hook it with her dorsal fin. The other trainers could only tell Laura, "Well, Misty's just being herself."

Your Inner Nature

A dolphin does not try to be something it is not. There is power in being true to your own inner nature. You may even find that once you stop struggling against your limitations and acknowledge them, there are ways to make them work for you. If not, perhaps you can choose to change them. But it may be more important to change the way you look at them.

It may be that you don't feel good about yourself and, so, act either overly sub-missive, letting people take advantage of you, or defensive and controlling, so they won't know how insecure you are. Remember, even the people who appear most confident have fears and doubts; everyone does. The trick is to trust your inner nature—get to know yourself, maximize your strengths, recognize your limitations, and work with them. We are all different; not better or worse, just different.

Chances are, if you feel you are lacking in a certain area (and who doesn't?), it is largely a matter of your mind replaying negative messages. You can take any characteristic and call it good or bad. Are you too picky, or are you gifted with fine sensibilities? Are you boring, or are you gentle and soothing to be around? Are you a chatterbox, or are you vivacious and entertaining? Shine a positive light on yourself, and do the same for others in your life. When you see the best in people, they tend to rise to the occasion, and also see the best in you.

Part Two

MIND

HOW DO WE KNOW what we know? When we're born, we are little learning machines, full of potential, with a highly developed brain capable of processing complex information. We embark upon a lifelong process of absorbing messages from the world around us. Messages come to us through all our senses, and they come in many forms—from formal education, to how it feels to get a hug, to what happens when you pull the cat's tail. Some we receive passively; many we seek out. It would be hard to deny that humans are creatures of mind.

Upon encountering dolphins, people are often amazed at the sense of intelligence dolphins convey and immediately want to quantify it. We are excited by the possibilities for greater communion that we expect to come from interaction with a highly intelligent creature. It has been especially exciting to encounter intelligence in a creature of the sea, an unexpected phenomenon. We have begun to think of dolphins as creatures of mind.

So, how does a dolphin's mind work? How do you answer the thousands of tantalizing questions raised by consideration of that one question? You can begin by observing dolphin behavior, as researchers have done with both captive and wild dolphins for barely fifty years. Since observation can take you only so far, the next step is to begin asking the dolphins questions, and observing how they answer. Researchers continue to come up with better and better ways to ask dolphins questions, and interpret their answers, but we are a long way from understanding what goes on in the mind of a dolphin. The more we learn, the more fascinating the study of dolphin intelligence becomes.

Some of the people who get to know dolphins best are trainers, the people who work with dolphins on a day-to-day basis and have a chance to interact with individual dolphins in all kinds of situations, reacting to each other, to their environment, to puzzles presented to them, as well as reacting to each trainer's personality. A good trainer has a strong sense of how a dolphin learns, how it displays its curiosity and creativity. Some of this information is not quantifiable, and yet all these clues lead us in the direction of understanding how a dolphin's mind works.

INTELLIGENCE

ONE OF THE FIRST questions visitors to the Dolphin Research Center ask is, "How intelligent are dolphins?" It's a good question insofar as it has led researchers to investigate a dolphin's mental abilities. It's a bad question if we are trying to determine how "good" dolphins are, the way we place value judgments on people's abilities based on their scores on our currently inadequate I.Q. tests. Most of the time, it is asked with a certain seeking after kinship, as in, "How like us are they?"

Even among our own species, intelligence manifests itself in different ways. Some people are more visually oriented, some more language oriented; some minds are

Above: Dana Carnegie with dolphin friends at the Dolphin Research Center.

more practical, some more theoretical. Intelligence is not a single thing, rather it refers to a wide range of abilities and skills. A person may be word smart, number smart, picture smart, nature smart, or people smart. We don't excel at measuring human intelligence, let alone the intelligence of another species, such as dolphins.

Up until fairly recently, few people doubted that "Man" was the center of the universe, the reason for it all, the ruler of the dumb beasts placed here to serve. In recent years, scientists have been more willing to allow that non-human animals have intelligence. Now, researchers have taken a new interest in the mental processes of animals, partially in an effort to discover clues for helping to reach non-verbal humans, such as children with certain mental disabilities, but also to satisfy the curiosity of humans who want to know the meanings behind things.

Intelligence is an important adaptive mechanism for many animals; those individuals who can solve problems in their world are more likely to survive to leave offspring for the next generation. Intelligence can be defined as the use of cognitive, or thinking, skills in learning to adapt to one's environment. Human cognitive skills include problem-solving ability, vocabulary and language skills, non-verbal communication skills, creativity, and the ability to conceptualize abstract concepts. Learning ability is considered to include the understanding of new concepts, and the degree to which those concepts can be applied to novel situations. Generalization of learning is said to take place when, for example, a child who has learned to avoid a hot stove also avoids other objects which might be hot enough to burn.

All in all "intelligence" is a term best applied to humans; we can, however, strive to understand a dolphin's cognitive abilities. One doesn't have to spend much time around dolphins to suspect that they are adept at learning new things and dealing with new situations, that they are creative, that they have great mental acuteness and comprehension. So how does one prove that? The approach researchers have taken is to present dolphins with problems in a controlled situation, and see how they solve them.

Dolphins Comprehending Human Language

Since part of the definition of intelligence has to do with the generalization of learning new situations, it may be that greater insight is gained by giving dolphins tests that are foreign to their experience, rather than observing them in their natural environment. Some of the best known and most important research has been done at the University of Hawaii's Kewalo Basin Marine Mammal Laboratory, where Dr. Louis Herman and a staff of graduate students have studied dolphins' problem-solving abilities since the late 1970s by attempting to teach them simple human language.

The results of this ongoing research have been quite remarkable. Dolphins have succeeded in learning vocabulary, communicated to them by hand signals or computer-generated tones. They have demonstrated that they can learn to understand our rules of grammar by responding to sentences as long as five words.

When researchers would give a dolphin a sentence such as, "Take frisbee to basket," the dolphin would perform the appropriate action. "Take basket to frisbee," would, of course, mean something different. There were paddles the dolphins could press to indicate either a "yes" or "no" answer, so that, when asked if there was a frisbee in the pool, they could indicate their understanding of the question.

The dolphins even invented appropriate responses to trick questions. When asked to take a frisbee to the basket when the basket had been removed from the pool, the dolphin responded by taking the frisbee (the direct object in the sentence) to the "no" paddle. When asked the same thing with no frisbee in the pool, the dolphin went directly to the "no" paddle. There was no training of these responses; the dolphins conceptualized them.

Dolphins appear to be able to generalize, which is a key facet in defining intelligence. Herman wondered how abstract a signal the dolphins would understand. Rather than a trainer standing before them, performing a hand signal, the dolphins were shown a TV monitor depicting the trainer—an eight-inch figure on a flat screen. They understood the signals immediately. The dolphins then saw only the trainer's arms and hands protruding through a dark backdrop, and the dolphins understood. Finally, they saw an image of white-gloved hands moving before a black background, and they still interpreted the signals correctly.

Though dolphins have demonstrated the mental capacity for understanding syntax and other elements of our language, they probably don't use it to communicate with one another. Researchers have found no evidence that dolphins use a language like ours, with words representing objects, actions, or concepts. But when given the opportunity, they learned it, despite the probability that it is different from anything they use in their daily lives. It is likely that an animal capable of such complexity of thought exercises this capacity in ways we have yet to comprehend. Perhaps they understand us better than we understand them. Dana Carnegie, publicity director at the Dolphin Research Center, says, "The dolphins are studying us every bit as much as we are studying them. It's just that they have us all figured out and we still have a lot of questions."

Metacognition—Do You Know When You Know?

A pertinent question relating to intelligence is whether a non-human can think on what people call a "conscious" level. Animal behavior has traditionally been assumed to be at an unconscious level—reacting according to pre-set genetic patterns, without awareness of the individual's own thoughts and feelings. A research study done at the Dolphin Research Center in 1991 by Jonathan Schull of Haverford College and David Smith of the New School for Social Research attempted to determine whether dolphins had metacognitive thought patterns, that is, did they have the ability to be conscious of their own thought processes.

Scientists study metacognition by presenting the subject (and this has been done with rats, people, rhesus monkeys, and dolphins) with a problem involving discrimination, in which some trials are easy to solve, but in other trials it becomes impossible to determine the right answer because the choices are so similar. The key is that the people and the monkeys knew when they reached the point where they couldn't tell the right answer, and would bail out and go on to an easier trial. They didn't guess, they knew when they didn't know. Rats put in a comparable situation were not aware of when it was impossible to know the answer and would just guess.

In the metacognition study at the Dolphin Research Center, dolphins were presented with an acoustic test designed to determine whether or not the dolphins were self-aware enough to know when the test became too difficult. In order for the dolphins to indicate their answers, basic training techniques were used to teach the dolphins to press one paddle when they heard a high tone, and a different paddle when they heard a low tone. This the dolphins learned easily enough. The real test came when the tone played was close to midway between high and low and was too difficult to identify as one or the other. Then, the dolphins could use a third paddle that allowed them to bail out and get an easier trial.

To the surprise of no one who worked with the dolphins, they learned to use all three paddles correctly. The way the dolphins responded to the trials demonstrated that they were aware when they were in doubt, and acted accordingly. They were aware of their own thought processes.

If dolphins "think about their thoughts" in a way comparable to our stream of consciousness, yet don't use words, how do they experience those thoughts? Are they capable of the negative self-talk that plagues people? How could they be, if they don't have words running through their minds? It would seem, rather, the dolphins' world is one of sound and pictures, which convey rich meaning to their agile minds.

Do You Think Too Much?

Our reasoning power can lead us astray. It is only one facet of who we are. Even dolphins can get stuck in a rut. During research, a dolphin may have difficulty thinking past what it has already tried. Then it's time for a break, for frolicking, for a change of pace. A fresh start often yields big leaps forward in solving the problem.

You may be worried about a problem. You try to think it through, but you're tired and you can't think. You sit at your desk and tell yourself, "I'm not moving until I think of what to do." You are trying too hard. If you go for a walk or play with the dog and shift your focus to what's happening around you in the moment, the answer may appear in your mind as if by magic.

What good is a complex mind if the rest of your being is out of balance? You may have a big project going on at work and forget to take care of yourself physically, spiritually, or emotionally. You are not paying attention to how you treat people, you get impatient with anything not directly related to your project, and your family life, friendships, or working relationships suffer. Your body responds by getting sick so you are forced to take a break. You feel adrift, cut off, and have difficulty finding your way back to your spiritual center.

This kind of behavior may stem from mental activity, but it sure isn't intelligence! At least not in the greater sense of successfully manipulating one's environment. Neglecting your body, heart, spirit, or relationships throws your life out of balance. If you find you are doing this, it's time to come down out of your head, at least a little bit, and give some energy to those areas of your being that are suffering. Instead of abusing your mental powers, use your mind as the marvelous tool that it is, to be developed, protected, and cherished.

TRAINING

RESEARCHERS WHO STUDY populations of wild dolphins in clear waters such as in the Bahamas or Shark Bay, Western Australia, have been able to observe individual dolphins year after year, learn which ones travel together and who is the mother of whom, watch how they relate to each other, and videotape and record their activities and sounds. Some researchers have become so familiar with particular dolphins, year after year, that they have established strong bonds of recognition and trust. They strive to interfere as little as possible with the dolphins' natural patterns of behavior.

Above: If it's not fun, it's not working. Here, a handler plays with Delphi and Kibby at the Dolphin Research Center.

This kind of contact is necessarily rare. Most observational research in the ocean waters is limited by poor visibility to surface observation, precluding insight into the behavior of dolphins underwater, where most of their behavior takes place. So many questions remain unanswered.

While observing dolphins' natural behavior in the long term may teach us a great deal about them, interacting with dolphins teaches us things that observation can't. Interacting with a dolphin in a training situation provides a window onto the inner world of the dolphin. This unique, playful relationship, based on respect and trust, can help build a bridge of understanding between our species.

From Susie's journal, June 1994:

In-water sessions with the dolphins are one of the most fun things I've ever had the privilege of doing. I can see myself standing on a rocky ledge by the fence in the front lagoon, with Florida Bay beyond. The water is up past my waist and A.J. is right in front of me. I hang the fish bucket on the post, put my whistle between my teeth, pick some seaweed out of my bathing suit, and give A.J. a wave signal. He wiggles his pec fin at me, I give a short tweet on the whistle and the session begins. I'm a handler, not a trainer, which means I don't usually train new behaviors and spend most of my work time in other areas at the Dolphin Research Center. But when I have a chance to do a session, I have a responsibility to maintain the signals that the dolphins know.

It's amazing how well they generalize signals from person to person—we try to be consistent, but can't be perfectly so. I think they learn not just what a dive signal looks like, but what each person's dive signal looks like. When students try out this kind of interaction with the dolphins, they often mangle the signals, but the dolphins usually get it anyway (unless it's Misty and she's playing dumb).

Other trainers have been working from docks in other areas of the lagoon while I work with A.J., and we always make a point of finishing at the same time. Otherwise, the dolphins who are done are likely to go distract those who aren't. In this case, the others let me know they're close to finishing and I ask A.J. to give me a pull back to the dock. What a companionable feeling, so close to this little dolphin, with my hand over the front of his dorsal fin as he swims to the dock towing me along. I haul out dripping onto the dock, exhilarated, surprised by gravity, and give A.J. the last fish in his bucket. We always show the dolphins when the buckets are empty, so if they do hang around after a session, we don't feel we're keeping them there under false pretenses. This time, A.J. is off like a shot, rejoining his gray-faced friends. I wonder if they talk about us. Thanks, A.J.

Building Bridges

Although initially, dolphin training may have been done for human entertainment, this does not describe a modern training environment. Most training today is done for one of five reasons: medical care, research, fun, exercise, and educating the public.

The training of medical behaviors facilitates the care of dolphins, and provides information which may be applicable to dolphins in the wild. Fortunately, dolphins have proven their ability to cooperate with medical procedures to an amazing degree. Dolphins have learned to voluntarily accommodate such procedures as swallowing a stomach tube to provide a sample of stomach fluids; sitting up at the dock, opening their mouths and swallowing vitamins or medication; floating in place next to a dock while an ultrasound is performed; opening the blowhole to allow a cotton swab to be inserted, which is used to make a slide analyzed for possible parasites; and providing samples of milk or saliva. The training paradigm allows trainers to communicate to the dolphins what they are trying to do. Once the dolphins understand, procedures that otherwise could be difficult or invasive are simple.

In training for research, dolphins learn the behaviors required by research protocols to study their mental or physical capabilities. Research studies are carefully designed to pose specific questions in such a way that the dolphins understand what is being asked and can provide answers.

Some training is just for mental and physical stimulation, in other words, for the dolphins' fun and exercise. To stay healthy, these naturally athletic animals need plenty of physical exercise and play. The vigorous behaviors that so delight human onlookers are also good for the dolphins.

At the Dolphin Research Center, visitors can observe dolphins participating in training sessions and gain a better appreciation of dolphins' mental and physical prowess. Many of the dolphins' natural behaviors are "captured" and paired with a signal. Visitors are amazed and delighted to see dolphins spiral through the water, imitate the actions of a human, or cooperate with a medical examination, all at the trainer's request. An appreciation of the dolphins is the "hook" that encourages people to conserve the marine environment.

At the Chicago Zoological Society's Dolphin Connection at Hawk's Cay Resort, similar routines were not only beneficial to the dolphins but educational and entertaining for the guests staying at the Resort. The entertainment factor which drew so many people to the sessions provided the perfect opportunity to convey messages about the Florida Keys marine environment and ways in which people could tailor their fun on the water to also ensure a healthy habitat for dolphins and other marine life.

A Training Session at the Dolphin Research Center

The trainer starts out at a dock in the dolphin's pool armed with a particular dolphin's symbol and the fish and vitamins allotted for that meal. The fish will be used in the training session as part of the reward system. The homemade symbols are made of wood and plastic tubing material and look like giant lollipops, each shaped differently: a circle, a square, a triangle, a crescent, a cross, and so on. Each of the dolphins at the Dolphin Research Center recognizes its own symbol—an easy thing for them to learn. The session begins with tapping underwater, then placing in the water the symbol that corresponds to the dolphin you're working with this session. In a typical session, the dolphins in the lagoon race to the docks, glance at the symbols, and either race by or, if they see their symbol, put on the brakes and sit up at the dock, hollering and splashing.

This is usually a high energy time, and the trainers give signals for high energy behaviors like high dives, spirals, back flips, and speed runs. Then, trainers and dolphins go on to the business of that session, perhaps practicing a medical behavior, or learning a new behavior for an upcoming research project. If members of the public are watching, there is plenty of showing off and demonstration of their skills and personalities.

For variety, a session may begin at the dock, but the trainer then slips into the water and goes to a shallow area of the pool where he or she can stand and give signals. It's a bit awkward for the trainer to travel around in the water holding a fish bucket, so often the dolphin will help by providing a dorsal pull. The dolphin then stations itself in the water and watches for a signal. The dolphins seem to get a huge kick out of in-water sessions, as do the trainers. Trainers make a point of introducing variety into sessions—working from boardwalks, beaches, boats or surfboards, and constantly inventing new challenges.

Communicating with dolphins in a training environment is an exciting and intimate experience—exciting, because of the vigor and brilliance that dolphins bring to the interaction, and intimate, because not only are the trainers required to put a great deal of themselves into the relationship, but in this setting, the dolphins can reveal so much of themselves.

How Does It Work?

So how does one begin? How can the dolphins even understand we are trying to tell them something or ask them questions?

Training of dolphins is based on the principles of operant conditioning, which include the fact that a rewarded behavior tends to be repeated. Behavior that is ignored tends to become "extinguished," or disappear. Complicated chains of behavior can be taught by leading the subject along in small steps, or increments.

When working with a dolphin, the first thing a trainer must do is establish rapport. The trainer spends time with individual animals, getting to know them, allowing them to get to know him or her, and building up a relationship based on trust. The dolphin begins to know what to expect from the human, and becomes comfortable with him or her—and vice versa.

For a reward-based system to work, the trainer must know what is rewarding for each individual dolphin. Some things are rewarding on a basic level, most notably food—a primary reinforcement for all species. Other things may become rewarding by learned association, for instance, money in itself is just a bit of paper or metal, but is rewarding for most people because we learn what it can bring us. This is called secondary reinforcement. For a dolphin, secondary reinforcements may be things it has learned to enjoy, such as applause, a favorite behavior, or playing with a certain object. Just as people have different likes and dislikes, not all dolphins find the same things rewarding, and the trainer must know the preferences of each dolphin to be successful.

In general, dolphin training involves showing the dolphin a hand signal or using a verbal signal that represents the desired behavior. Since differentiating sounds in air seems to be somewhat tricky for a dolphin (they have pin-hole ears with no external ear flap), hand signals are more common. Often, a hand signal is combined with a trainer calling out the behavior. Dolphins seem to reflect the energy put into the session by the trainer; thus the more upbeat the trainer, the more enthusiastic the dolphin. (This is just one of the ways in which the dolphins train the humans.)

Another necessary element of training is to communicate clearly to the subject. A dolphin who is trying to figure out a new signal may go through a series of movements in rapid succession, and it is impossible to get the reward to them at the exact moment the desired movement is taking place. So the trainer uses a short, distinct blast on a whistle, called the "bridge," to bridge the gap in time between the instant the desired behavior occurs and the time the reward is received. Dolphins listen for the whistle to tell them when they are getting it right, and can come back for their reward of fish, applause, or a back rub. It takes skill and precision to use the bridge correctly. If the whistle is sounded too early, too late, or inconsistently, the dolphin may be confused. The direction must be done succinctly, without mixed messages or hesitation, for the dolphin to understand what the trainer is asking it to do.

Workshop participants at the Dolphin Research Center experience what's called the training game. One member of the group acts as the "dolphin" and leaves the group while the rest choose a behavior to be taught. The required behavior may be something like jumping up and down on one foot or scratching your head with your right hand. Another group member acts as "trainer" and must convey to the "dolphin" the chosen behavior solely by means of bridging with a whistle. The difficulty—and fun—of doing this demonstrates how much both trainer and dolphin invest in the training relationship. One aspect that usually comes across quite clearly is the effect of frustration—if the trainer allows the dolphin to become frustrated, it's no longer fun, and learning starts to shut down. Both people and dolphins learn more easily when they are having fun—their minds are open, they are fully present, and ideas are flowing freely.

Using these basic methods, dolphins can learn incredibly complex procedures. When teaching a complex behavior, a trainer uses successive approximations—small steps that are learned gradually that lead in the direction of the desired result. Anyone who has worked closely with dolphins will tell you that training is very much a two-way street. Good trainers learn as they go along, and adapt their methods to the behavior of the dolphins. The trainer must be well prepared and willing to try different approaches, depending on the actions and reactions of the dolphin during a training session. The trainer figures out a behavior chain ahead of time in order to be flexible during the session itself and proceed to the next step if the dolphin is learning quickly, or shift gears if the approach is not working.

Once you have gained a dolphin's trust and have learned to communicate clearly in a training situation, you must be sure you are providing reachable goals for the dolphin to attain. You cannot ask or expect a particular dolphin to do more than it is capable of doing. Some dolphins learn more quickly than others, and some require more patience and time to reach the goal of learning a particular behavior. Different dolphins learn in different ways, and are better or worse at different types of behaviors. A good trainer respects these differences. This is all part of the training relationship, and provides a fascinating glimpse at the dolphins' capabilities and personalities.

For trainers, the bottom line seems to be that they continually learn more from the dolphins than they teach.

From Greg Jakush, Founder and President, Marine Animal Lifeline, Biddeford, Maine:

I had just started my job as a new dolphin trainer at the Dolphin Research Center. I practiced for days learning the hand signals, using the bridge, and focusing on how my body language would be critical in the communication between the dolphins and myself. I was extremely nervous but also very excited. I had my first solo session with the three boys—Natua, Delphi, and Kibby. It was a handful! Kibby was doing his typical impatient wandering around the pool and focusing on the girls next door; Delphi was doing a good job of ignoring me; and Natua was just hanging out at the dock watching me.

There was a tour group watching the session, and the Director of Training was behind me critiquing my performance. I was frazzled, unfocused, and frustrated. This continued for a while and then Natua disappeared. At that point, I thought my career as a dolphin trainer was over! However, Natua reappeared at the dock with a present—a rock from the bottom of the lagoon. He leaned over the edge of the dock and dropped it at my feet, continuing to watch me.

I'll never know what it was that made him do that, but it distracted me enough to take a moment and breathe. I took the rock, put it behind me and recalled Delphi and Kibby to the dock. Natua waited for me in his assigned spot. Delphi and Kibby came back, but only for a moment. I turned to Nat and signaled him to show off for the crowd. He rocketed into the air higher than I've ever seen and the crowd let out an enormous roar! Nat stole the show and bailed me out. He was watching me panic and for whatever reason, decided to present me with the gift of the rock. I received it as a message: Things may not always go the way you plan. So just relax, take a breath, accept what's going on and move with it. But above all…just have fun! Because it will all be OK.

Training Techniques Work for All of Us

Hawk's Cay Resort and Marina is chosen as a destination by many businesses both as a reward for their top employees and to conduct training seminars for their future successes. Hawk's Cay is also home to a colony of bottlenose dolphins, which provide daily opportunities for trainers to answer questions about dolphins for people from all over the world.

A sales group from a Texas real estate firm asked the Chicago Zoological Society Dolphin Connection trainers to talk to the group about dolphin training techniques and how they might relate to their business environment. It was a natural: The first principle made clear to the sales managers was the necessity for building rapport with the dolphins and establishing trust, just as these managers have to do with their sales force. Then it is necessary to communicate clearly, without mixed messages or confusion, and make sure that the dolphins or humans know what is expected. Goals must be clear and attainable; you should not ask the impossible of either dolphin or human.

Rewarding a dolphin for doing a good job is comparable to the essential element of recognizing the accomplishments of an employee or co-worker. People like to be patted on the back and told they are doing a good job. This gives them the encouragement and incentive to reach further, accomplish more, and go beyond what they imagined. Positive reinforcement works wonders, whether you want to teach a child to clean her room, teach a dolphin to dive on cue, or teach an employee to get to meetings on time. It is, of course, necessary to know what is motivating for each individual, since we are all different in this respect. Finally, not only is it OK to enjoy what you are doing, it's essential for good health and happiness, not to mention good results.

Earn trust and respect, communicate clearly, set goals, don't ask for more than can be delivered, reward a job well done, exercise your sense of humor, and find time to relax and play—it works for the dolphins, and it can work for people, too.

CURIOSITY & CREATIVITY

Bottlenose dolphins, gregarious enough by nature to be able to fit into a life around humans, often seem interested in the challenges we present them. We learned a great deal about a dolphin's potential for curiosity and creativity from Natua, who was born in 1974 at the facility that was to become the Dolphin Research Center. From the beginning, Nat was as fascinated by humans as they were by him, and seemed to take great delight in figuring out their games. This curiosity, combined with an extremely patient and flexible personality, made Nat a perfect subject for research projects. Although research sessions are usually designed

Above: Kelly Jane Rodriguez with a friend at the Dolphin Research Center—children and dolphins have much in common.

around fish rewards, Nat often gave the distinct impression that he was more interested in the problem than the reward.

Most people like mental challenges and become bored without them. Imagine if you couldn't read a book, work a crossword puzzle, take apart an engine, practice a piece of music, or whatever it is you do for mental stimulation. Wild dolphins devote 80 percent of their time to the demands of survival, such as foraging and catching their food, and avoiding predators. Dolphins in human care have these requirements taken care of for them, and so turn their minds to other things. The dolphins appear to become bored if not challenged, and will make up games to amuse themselves, or learn with enthusiasm those puzzles presented to them by people. Trainers find that dolphins do not like constant repetition and are much more motivated to figure out something new.

Innovate

Dolphins at the Dolphin Research Center and elsewhere learn a type of behavior the trainers have dubbed "innovate." They are shown a new hand signal, one for which they have not learned a meaning. Usually in this situation, they will start "guessing" and looking for clues, that is, trying things to see what brings a positive response from the trainer. They may wave a pectoral fin or offer any one of a number of familiar behaviors, and be rewarded. They are shown the same signal again, and may try what worked before, but are not rewarded. They have learned that the first behavior no longer works. What the trainer is looking for is a series of behaviors all different from each other. They are shown the signal several times in a row, and are supposed to do something different each time. It can be anything—a familiar behavior, or something they make up on the spot—as long as it's different from anything they have done in this sequence. It's amazing that the dolphins get this concept—would people "get it" as quickly? The results can be hilarious, with dolphins snorting, splashing, spinning, flipping, and blowing bubbles from their blowholes as they run through their repertoires.

Some dolphins invented long chains of behavior, and in each session in which they were shown the "innovate" signals, they would rehearse the same series, like a choreographed routine! Some would get hung up on the same few behaviors; some would combine known behaviors in creative ways—swimming belly up and spitting water, for instance. Many of these creations the trainers liked so much, they came up with new signals for them, so they could ask for them on cue.

Imitate

Dolphins are naturally imitative, and mimic not only the behavior and sounds of other dolphins, but that of humans and other animals as well. They even learn to do this on signal; they are taught a hand signal that represents the concept of imitating, and will watch the trainer, or some other person (or people) the trainer designates, and imitate what they are doing. Of course, it has to be something of which they are physically capable. If you splash water at them, they splash water at you. If you wave at them, they wave at you. If you rotate in a circle, they do the same. Sometimes, visitors participating in this game will stand on one leg, or scratch their head, which shows how hard it is to grasp the capabilities and limitations of another species.

One trainer, working with Kibby and trying out some new ideas, showed him the signal for "imitate," then laid flat on the floating dock with her feet sticking up, thinking maybe he would go head down in the water and stick his flukes up, a behavior the dolphins know on signal. Kibby seemed confused, swimming around, staring at her, and finally, to her great surprise and some consternation, popped his five-hundred pound body out of the water onto the floating dock! The trainer figures Kibby realized she was lying on the dock and thought maybe that was what she wanted him to imitate.

Dolphin imitating trainer at the Dolphin Research Center.

Dolphins Meeting People's Special Needs

Dolphin-human therapy at the Dolphin Research Center involves dolphins and staff working with adults and children with various mental or physical disabilities, and has yielded many amazing stories of dolphin creativity. The dolphins have an uncanny ability to analyze a person's special needs, and come up with a successful approach. They often echolocate on the person in the water with them and can identify something special about that person relating to physical disability, such as metal in the body or bones that have healed. Dolphins are exquisite observers, and probably also pick up on any unusual body language. But why they are so motivated and how they come up with appropriate strategies in these therapy sessions remains a mystery. Although the sessions take place with a therapist and dolphin trainer, much of what the dolphins contribute is not trained.

One morning, the dolphin in the program was Annessa, a young female dolphin born at the Dolphin Research Center. The participant was a young boy whose disability left him with no strength whatsoever in his neck. His head hung limply against his chest unless supported by a brace. He couldn't move his head side to side and couldn't even stick out his tongue.

The dolphin's role in a therapy session is often to provide both stimulation and motivation. The object of the session that morning was to teach the boy to identify items pictured on square boards. If he correctly identified the pictures, his reward would be to interact in the water with Annessa. What the boy wanted to do, more than anything else, was to get a dorsal pull through the water from a dolphin, holding on to the base of the curved fin on the dolphin's back.

You could see the determination and concentration on the boy's face as he responded to each of the boards, getting every one of them correct. At a signal from the trainer, Annessa swam right up alongside the boy, ready to provide him his treat. Unfortunately, the boy couldn't turn his head to see where Anna was, or where to place his hand to hold on to her. The trainers were wondering what to do to make it work.

With no instructions from anyone, and having never done so before, Annessa somehow sized up the situation, sidled up a little closer to and just forward of where she would normally stop, turned slightly on her side, and made eye contact with the boy. Then she gave him her pectoral fin, or side flipper, and pulled him around in the water like that. The boy's smile lit up the scene and brought tears to the eyes of everyone there. The trainer was heard to say, "What the heck are we here for? The dolphins teach us more than we could ever teach them!"

Creative Feeding Strategies

One of the most obvious ways in which dolphins display their adaptive creativity is in their methods of getting food. Dolphins are opportunistic feeders, meaning they will take a meal wherever and however they can get it! When Ken Norris first started observing wild bottlenose dolphins in San Diego Bay in the 1950s, he discovered they were on a fairly regular daily routine. During part of the day they would follow the ferry, presumably feeding in the muck turned up by the ship's passage. They would also follow a Navy garbage scow along the coast, feeding on the fish attracted to the garbage. These dolphins had adapted to life in a busy port.

Bottlenose dolphins inhabiting the Indian River Lagoon system in Florida are well known to the local blue crab fishermen as pests who follow their boats to feed on discarded bait fish. The dolphins also apparently engage in "crab pot tipping," in which they break into the baited traps to steal the tasty herring or menhaden. The fishermen have cooperated with researchers studying this behavior to come up with a more effective method for securing the door of the traps to deter the dolphins. Crab pot tipping is not without risk for the dolphins: casualties have been found, the dead dolphins having become entangled in the crab pot buoy lines.

Dolphins at Shark Bay, Australia, have been filmed "hydroplaning" parallel to the beach in a few inches of water to confound and catch their prey, though it seems relatively few of the dolphins in this area have perfected this particularly difficult skill. Ten years of observational research at Shark Bay reveals that not only do dolphins develop their own styles of foraging, but distinctive methods are passed down from mothers to their calves, particularly female calves. A few dolphins are known as sponge-foraging dolphins—they pull up a mass of sponge and hold it in their mouths so that it covers the tip of their rostra (snouts). It's not known exactly how they use this apparent tool, but researchers thought it might serve to protect their snouts as the dolphins foraged along the bottom.

The Shark Bay dolphins also show up for handouts from people who gather from all over the world to see them, orchestrated by locals who have learned to know the individual dolphins well. While this is a great delight to the visitors, it indicates a dark side to dolphins' talent for seeking out an easy food source: people who feed wild dolphins may seriously interfere with the dolphins' ability to develop more natural foraging techniques, risk accidentally hurting them because of close contact with boat propellers or entanglement in fishing gear, or make the dolphins sick from giving them bad fish.

Wild dolphins don't normally eat dead fish, and dolphins in human care are provided only the highest quality fish that is flash frozen, then thawed with extreme care. Instead of following fish that move about seasonally, dolphins may opt for staying in an area where they have come to expect boats with people that will feed them. Then the people disappear, and the dolphins are left in difficulty. Meanwhile, calves may not be learning important hunting skills.

For all these reasons, it is now illegal to feed wild dolphins in the United States. Unfortunately, it still occurs; in fact, in some areas, both commercially operated and recreational boats go out to "swim with" the wild dolphins, in a melee of boats, personal watercraft, dolphins, and people. Both dolphins and people ignore the dangers of fishing line and hooks in the water, and active boat traffic. Dolphins have been horribly mutilated. Misguided people are either unaware of or unconcerned with both the laws and the danger.

On some occasions, frustrated dolphins have been known to injure swimmers. For instance, a tourist boat that had conditioned dolphins in the area to gather around and compete for the fish thrown from it would also allow swimmers in the water, feeding dolphins by hand. When the boat showed up with no fish, and tourists got in the water with the dolphins who had gathered to beg for fish, one dolphin displayed its annoyance by whacking a woman with its tail flukes, causing serious injury.

In our eagerness to relate to another being, in this case dolphins, people are ignoring the damage they can do. Whether relating to dolphins or to people, it is important to examine both your motives and your methods, and consider the impact you are having on the recipient of your attentions. Do you assume because the interaction makes you happy that it is the same for them?

Outsmarting Yourself

The dolphins are clever enough to take advantage of an easy food source, but are misled into ignoring their normal feeding habits. It is possible to outsmart yourself, particularly if you get out of touch with the natural rhythms of your existence.

Let's say you are working so you can support yourself, and perhaps a family, and can buy the things you need and want. You get by on what you make, you enjoy your family and friends, you spend time on hobbies and recreation—you are happy. But, you think, if only you had more money, you'd be even happier. There is pressure at work for you to put in longer hours. You sign up for overtime, you get more involved with your job, you fret over promotions. You are more tense and harder to get along with, and have less time for leisure or other pursuits. Someday, you think, when I'm really well off financially, I'll be able to take that dream vacation, I'll be able to spend more time with my spouse and rebuild our relationship, I'll get back to that hobby, I'll get back in shape. Then I'll be happy.

The mistake is that you're postponing happiness. Perhaps with a simpler lifestyle you wouldn't have as much spending money, but you would have time for doing the things that made you happy in the first place. You think you need a lot of money to spend on a vacation? Visualize what aspects of that trip would make you happy, and imagine how you can make them happen now, closer to home. Use your creativity, and don't limit yourself to what you've done in the past.

Artistic creativity is a special blessing or curse, depending on what stage of the process you are in. We create because we can, because the inspiration comes to us, and, if we are listening, we act on it. We have skillful hands and active minds to accompany our natural curiosity. This is one kind of creativity, but not the only one. Creativity can be applied to many areas of everyday life.

Dolphins use their intelligence to make the most of their environment, to relate creatively with others, and to have fun. Consequently, we are struck with admiration for the sense of freedom and joy they convey. Perhaps the secret of owning that joy and freedom lies in applying our intelligence and creativity to connecting with the world around us, to finding mental challenges we enjoy, to awakening our curiosity every day, and to relating creatively to the people, and animals, with whom we share our lives.

Part Three

BODY

IF YOU THINK of dolphins as ethereal, you probably haven't been very close to a dolphin. Dolphins are vigorous animals; their physical energy is electric. Even at rest, a dolphin conveys a powerful physical presence.

It is impossible to describe a dolphin without considering how it moves through the physical world. How exciting it is to witness a sharp mind operating in such a beautiful, strong, and graceful body! The adaptations that allow a dolphin to survive so well as a marine mammal are complex. A dolphin's physical characteristics have everything to do with how it relates to the environment and to others of its kind.

MOVEMENT

IF YOU'RE LUCKY enough to have seen dolphins speeding effortlessly through the water, you've witnessed the grace and skill with which they move through their world. It has taken many millions of years of evolution for dolphins to achieve their current state of beautiful adaptation as fully marine mammals. The prevailing theory among most scientists is that dolphins began their evolutionary history as a more typical four-legged land mammal, probably sharing an ancestor with today's hippopotamus. What a long, complex path that animal would have had to take to become the graceful, streamlined dolphin of today!

Above: Power and agility—Rainbow and Sandy, adult male dolphins at the Dolphin Research Center, in coordinated back dives.

A dolphin has horizontal tail flukes that it moves up and down when it swims, unlike fish, which have a vertical tail that moves side to side. There are no bones in the stationary dorsal fin on the top of a dolphin's back, which provides stability, or in the tail flukes, which flex up and down controlled by ligaments. Heavy bands of muscle run down the dolphin's back and sides into its lower body and tail stock. The stiff tail stock or "caudal keel" is perpendicular to the flukes, and flattened like a double-edged sword. This arrangement can send a dolphin slicing through the water at speeds of twenty-five miles per hour, as well as hurtling out of the water in leaps and spirals.

An x-ray of a dolphin's pectoral fin, or flipper, reveals most of the same bones that we have in our arms and hands, with short, flat humerus, radius, and ulna, and long finger bones. A ball and socket joint allows a dolphin subtle movements of the pectoral fins it can use for stabilizing itself or to steer—with the slightest adjustments, it can change direction, turn upside down, or rotate off in a spin. Dolphins in facilities use their pectoral fins to wave and "clap" in imitation of human movements, and will sometimes cruise by a dock, rolling on one side with a pectoral fin extended to give a human friend a "high five." Their pectoral fins feel strong; they are flat and smooth, and flexible at the trailing edges which thin out and may be characterized by little notches or curves unique to that individual dolphin.

Dolphins are designed for forward movement; they have difficulty back-peddling, although they may do so if the situation demands it. They can move their heads side-to-side, as they may do when echolocating on an object in front of them, but their spines are not flexible enough to allow them to bend their heads around to their tails. Having lost many of the gawky joints that we possess, they lack our range of physical expression, but the elegant movement of dolphins is perfectly suited to their lifestyle—no superfluous gestures to interfere as they slip through the fluid medium of their environment.

Dolphins do have a certain repertoire of gestures and can convey a great deal through body language that even we can detect. A widened eye may convey curiosity, a roll of the eye convey fear, or a half-closed eye, a sexy mood; amorous dolphins can be seen nuzzling, stroking with pectoral fins, or raking with teeth, as well as violently rolling and thrashing about. A sharp slap of the flukes or pectoral fin on the water's surface may be a warning or rebuke. Poking or ramming with the hard snout (rostrum) is an aggressive act that can chase off or kill an attacking shark.

Dolphins, with that streamlined shape (after which we've modeled our torpedoes) can propel themselves out of the water in an awesome spiral. Spinner dolphins get their name from the frequency of this activity. There is a theory that this behavior serves the pod by providing sound markers as the dolphins splash back into the water, helping to orient the traveling group, which may consist of hundreds of dolphins. We see the spiral dive and are impressed by its power.

As strong and vigorous as they are, dolphins have exquisite control over their bodies. Sitting up vertically with their heads poked out of the water is called spy-hopping, and seems to be how they survey the scene above the water's surface. Wild spotted dolphins have been observed in the clear waters of the Bahamas with their heads down, flukes up, rostrums a few inches from the sandy bottom, echolocating to find tasty eels or flounder hidden in the sand. In interacting with humans, a trained dolphin can move ever so gently, bringing that hard rostrum next to a delicate human cheekbone for a "kiss."

Lest we elevate dolphins to a divine status that we cannot attain, realize that dolphins sometimes crash, sometimes run into each other by accident, sometimes make hilarious miscalculations. The beauty of it is that they don't seem to worry about looking foolish.

As people go to visit the dolphins' watery home, they are at first weighted down by gravity, whether it be on the deck of a boat, or a floating dock in a lagoon or pool. Entering the water, they are freed from the strain of that downward pull and can experience the buoyancy in which dolphins spend their whole lives. Depending on their level of experience and swimming ability, people may at this point feel tense and awkward, even fearful in an unfamiliar environment. When dolphins approach, the people soon lose their self-consciousness as the energy of the dolphins pulls them into the experience of the moment.

Elegance in motion—Wild spotted dolphins in the tranquil waters of the Bahamas.

Wayne "Scott" Smith, The Dolphin Dream Team

From Susie's journal, August, 1992:

I can see myself underwater, swimming in the front lagoon with A.J. and Santini. The water is murky, so their shapes appear and disappear like ghosts. My head is filled with the sound of their echolocation—I experience it as a buzzing at the base of my skull. Not unpleasant, but weird. It's as though the water is crackling with the electricity of their powerful presence. I am in their medium, and I feel so awkward and slow by comparison. Wearing a snorkel, I have to surface to breathe, but how clumsy I am compared to their rapid, graceful movements and quick blows.

This is a "free swim"—we are not trying to control or teach or ask questions. We don't touch the dolphins underwater so we don't risk starting something we can't finish in the way of sexual behavior. The dolphins have come to understand how fragile we are and behave appropriately during training and therapy sessions, but that interaction takes place on the surface. Beneath the surface it is different; we are in their realm, and it is for us to behave appropriately. I watch. I swim.

The dolphins swim close beside me, accepting, interested. To be in the water with the dolphins is to have an overwhelming sense of their power in a way not possible from a dock or boat. They have amazing control over their bodies. Their energy feels pure and primal, yet they can be so careful with us.

The young dolphins seem to like it when I try to swim fast and will stay back with me for a little while, then burst forward, as if they are trying to wait for me but they just can't move that slowly. I swim as fast as I can and they literally swim circles around me. What a way to move! When I can't see them, I can still hear them, buzzing, clicking, whistling. A.J. appears in front of me, materializing out of the murk, eyeballs me for a timeless moment, and, with the slightest flick of his tail flukes, is gone.

There is something about the quality of the dolphins' movement, the way their energy feels to us, that for centuries has had great appeal. Perhaps it is because they seem so easy in their world—so graceful, so strong, so adept. It seems a simpler way to be; it would be fun to be a dolphin and go rocketing through the waters with a flick of the tail, or float suspended on the surface, buoyed by the water, at home in the sea. Of course, for a real dolphin, there are such difficulties as finding food, protecting the young, avoiding fishing nets and pollution, and fighting off sharks—but to us, dolphins represent peace and harmony. We admire them, and would like to feel that way inside our own skins—harmonious, fluid, powerful.

Body Wisdom

So often we feel weighted down: by gravity, by our jobs, by our responsibilities. In our society, where so many work at desks, sit at computers, stand in schoolrooms, care for hospital patients, work on assembly lines, or hurry around restaurants waiting on tables, it is easy for busy people to forget what they are doing to their bodies. We heedlessly pour our energy down the drain, or funnel energy to mental problems. We lose connection with our physical being. This separation can cause physical illness, mental anxiety, and spiritual chaos. If you long to feel easy in your world, it may be time for you to reconnect with your body.

When's the last time you floated? Look for an opportunity to float in water—in a swimming pool, an ocean, lake, river, or even a big tub. It gives you a different sense of your body and of the space in which you live. Spend some time concentrating on the sensations against your skin. What would it be like to be a dolphin, in constant motion, subject to water pressure but not the gravity that ties us to the land?

Dolphins are never really stationary. They live in a suspended state, buoyed by water, subject to the movement of waves and currents. What are the qualities of movement in your world? Can you make yourself aware of the wind in the trees, the direction the rain is falling, the solid ground on which you stand, the Earth turning under your feet?

While there is a time to sit quietly and meditate, rest, or pray, the sacred traditions of many cultures connect dance or rituals of movement with worship as well. In Native American traditions, the spiral is a symbol of sacred forces that can whirl you into the center of being. Masters in some Sufi traditions practice a ritualized whirling dance in order to connect with the source of being. Get up and move your body. Dolphins call you to the dance.

SENSUALITY

DOLPHINS ARE SENSUOUS animals—they are not shy about gratification of the senses. They perceive their world through excellent eyesight, although they probably don't see in color (there is relatively little color in the underwater world, past the shallower depths). They don't have a sense of smell, but they do have a sense of taste, and who knows what messages they are able to pick up from the water around them as they taste their world? (Trainers in dolphin facilities tell many stories of the preference of individual dolphins for certain kinds of fish, cut in certain ways, and how dolphins train their trainers to "jump through hoops" to get them to eat.)

Above: A sensuous interlude—Nat and Misty at the Dolphin Research Center.

Their hearing is far better than ours, and works in combination with their primary sense of echolocation. Dolphins have sensitive skin, and, although they don't have fingers like we do, touch is an important part of their lives. They spend a lot of time in close physical contact, and seem to engage in sexual activity just for fun.

And they certainly appeal to our senses. What a treat to stroke a dolphin's skin—it feels very firm and silky smooth. Bottlenose dolphins are unusual mammals in that the only hair to be found on them is in the form of whiskers on the snout of a new-born calf, which quickly fall out and are not replaced. So, while a calf has hair as it develops in its mother's womb, there is no hair on an adult bottlenose dolphin—only smooth, sleek skin. If you're close enough, you can see the tiny ridges in a dolphin's skin that run across its back. These ridges contribute to the flow of water around its streamlined form as the dolphin swims—there is very little turbulence as they glide through the water.

Sometimes you can feel and see dark gray skin sloughing off, if a dolphin has not been active enough for it to slough off naturally or through rubbing against others. The top layer of dolphins' skin is shed and replaced much faster than ours—they can go through a layer of epidermis every couple of hours; it takes us a couple of days. Again, this physiological adaptation means less resistance as they swim.

Dolphins in facilities often show a fondness for back rubs. When they're in the mood, they will glide by within reach or come up under an outstretched hand. Some dolphins even seem to enjoy having their tongues tickled. The dolphin pokes its head above the surface and opens its mouth, moving its tongue forward against your hand as you rub it.

It's apparent that dolphins enjoy being touched, and that touching and being touched has social content as well. A touch conveys different information depending on where and how the touch is given, and dolphins touch each other regularly in various ways, such as stroking with pectoral fins, and poking or nuzzling with the rostrum. It is likely that touching plays an important part in dolphin communication, although we do not clearly understand its meaning.

From Major's journal, the Bahamas, July 5, 1994:

The word for the day was tactile, tactile, tactile! Stub and Stubette, a male and female with dorsal fins shortened through interspecies tussles or possibly shark attacks, were especially tactile and gave me my first side-to-side touch with wild dolphins. They initiated the contact and certainly appeared to want more and more of it. They definitely recognize Denise and hang around her all the time.

Among themselves, dolphins are constantly rubbing against each other with pec fins, dorsals, rostrums, and every other body part, including the entire body.... Several were seen actually copulating, and there was constant body posturing.

Responsible programs that include swimming with dolphins, whether in facilities or in the wild, will caution you that your body language (such as floating in what could be interpreted as a submissive posture) or touch (they are very sensitive on the

underside) could trigger a sexual response that could be overwhelming, even danger-
ous. An adult bottlenose dolphin may weigh six hundred to eight hundred pounds,
has a rostrum hard as a baseball bat, and up to one hundred pointed, conical teeth.
Its muscular tail can propel it fifteen or more feet out of the water. During sexual
activity, dolphins commonly rake each other with their teeth, leaving sometimes
bloody parallel scratches. They thrash and whirl, churning up a maelstrom of water.

Yet, with all this raw power, dolphins do learn what is appropriate in interacting
with delicate humans, and can contain their power with great finesse. They can
temper their natural sensuousness and exhibit amazing self-control. Dolphins show
great sensitivity to differences in people, even to the point of recognizing the abilities of healthy people in the water with them for fun, and people with disabilities
who need to connect in a gentler way.

The Need for Physical Contact

Human beings need physical touch; babies thrive on cuddling and touching, and
can suffer physically and emotionally when lacking physical contact. Complexities of
our societies confuse this issue considerably, and people are raised with widely varying degrees of physical interaction. We have bumper stickers to remind people to
hug their children! School teachers refrain from physical contact with their young
charges for fear of their touches being misinterpreted by parents. Yet, we all have
an innate need to be touched and many people don't get enough simple physical

contact. Touching and being touched is healthy and as important to our mental and physical well-being as eating and sleeping.

As young children, we are at home in our bodies. Babies explore their own bodies with wonder and discovery. Children run, jump, dance, and touch unselfconsciously. Not all families encourage this physicality and may even punish it. Sometimes as people grow to adulthood, they get out of touch with their own bodies, or become uncomfortable with physical contact.

Dolphins apparently suffer no such complications. In studying spinner dolphins in the Pacific, Dr. Ken Norris and his students observed that touching and mating took place in cycles, between various individuals, apparently as a way of reconnecting, especially when an individual was rejoining a group. Dolphin society is dynamic, and an individual may travel with one sub-group, then rejoin another; physical contact is a critical part of the bonds that hold their society together.

Setting Boundaries

Dolphins also are good at communicating when they don't want to be touched. Some behaviors, such as tail slapping, and jaw popping, may be used to indicate that touching would be unwelcome at that time. Responsible programs that involve wild dolphin interactions are careful to respect the preferences of individual dolphins, as expressed through their body language. While wild dolphins may approach people to interact, that doesn't mean they want to be touched by strangers.

According to Captain Wayne "Scott" Smith of the Dolphin Dream Team, who has been interacting with and recording the behaviors of Atlantic spotted dolphins of the Little Bahama Bank since 1981: "It is important to remember that these are wild dolphins; they come of their own free will because they are curious and friendly. Of the 120 dolphins in the area, there are only about five that like to be touched." The Dream Team literature instructs program participants: "Please don't try and touch them; just swim and dive, and if you're very lucky, one of them may just touch you."

If we can be as sensitive to each other, we can know when to enjoy the relaxed physical contact that draws us closer, and when to respect people's boundaries. Children are sometimes better at expressing their preferences than adults—they know when they want to be held and when they want to stand alone. This is natural; it's OK to express your wishes and expect others to respect them. In fact, the more comfortable you are in doing this, the less likely you are to wait until you are really uncomfortable and end up snapping at someone who, unfortunately, couldn't read your mind. Recognizing that you don't always have to be available may increase your enjoyment of the times when you do want to feel physically connected with your world and the people with whom you share it.

BREATH

Nothing about dolphins is more distinctive than the breath. As marine mammals, the breathing of air with lungs represents the interface between their world and ours. Conceived in the water, born in the water, they eat, mate, rest, and play in the water. But while under water, they hold their breath and must come to the surface for air.

Bottlenose dolphins generally breathe every few minutes or a couple of times a minute, depending on the activity in which they are engaged. The length of time between breaths varies. The dolphins must decide when to take each breath. Research

Above: At the water's surface, Aleta, Merina and Santini show their blowholes.

has demonstrated that they can learn to hold their breath for up to fifteen minutes, although since this species hunts for food in fairly shallow water, they don't ordinarily need to do so.

A human baby is born from a fluid world into a world of light and air, and must clear its lungs in order to take its first breath. So, too, a dolphin calf, immediately upon its birth into a watery world, must make its way to the surface for that first breath of air. It is usually helped in this critical effort by its mother or by a mid-wife dolphin, another adult female who attends the birth. From then on, it must surface periodically for the explosive exhale and rapid inhale that characterize a dolphin's breathing pattern.

Conscious Breathing

A dolphin doesn't breathe through its mouth, only through the blowhole at the top of its head. The mouth leads to the esophagus which goes to the dolphin's stomach; the blowhole opens the nasal passage to its lungs. The location of the blowhole allows a dolphin to breath without having to bring its whole head out of the water. (Imagine yourself swimming; to get air, you have to turn your head until your face is out of the water; if your nose were at the back of your head, you could simply rise and break the surface to breathe—a far more elegant system.) The blowhole is covered by a muscular flap of tissue that is closed when relaxed, and pulls aside when the dolphin consciously opens the blowhole to breathe.

Humans are involuntary breathers; we breathe without thinking about it. We can undergo anesthesia or be knocked unconscious, yet we continue to breathe. Dolphins lack this ability; they must have some degree of consciousness to breathe. So how do dolphins sleep? This is a common question. Although not all scientists agree on the answer, a popular theory is that when a dolphin rests, it "shuts down" only half of its brain, allowing it to remain conscious enough to breathe. It may be that dolphins don't need to sleep like terrestrial mammals because their bodies are not subject to the constant strain of gravity.

During periods of rest, pods of dolphins can be observed "barging" or floating like logs on the water's surface. This is a quiet time punctuated by the hypnotizing "te-puuhh-kiihh" of the dolphins' exhalation and inhalation. Sometimes you may even hear some snorting or coughing from the blowhole, if a dolphin has congestion in its lungs, or just accidentally got water in its "nose"!

Complete Breathing

Remarkably adapted to life in a marine environment, dolphins' breath is more efficient than ours. With each breath, they exchange much more of the air volume in their lungs, and their muscle tissue stores more oxygen so it can be available quickly when needed by the vital organs, particularly in situations where they are submerged for long periods of time. Since they can't breathe underwater, being able to hold their breath for extended periods of time may be vital if they are busily engaged in catching their dinner, or eluding a predator. The fact that their mouths do not lead to their lungs allows them to capture and swallow fish without affecting their breathing. It also makes sense that, when they do breathe, the breath be deep and rapid, to avoid getting water in their blowhole, especially when traveling at high speeds.

Dolphins teach us about conscious, complete breathing. Unless we are swimming and, like the dolphins, have to surface for air, we are usually unconscious of our breathing—it is reflexive. Most people have a habit of rather shallow breathing. When we're tense, we tend to hold our breath. Yet, we cannot go without oxygen for more than a few minutes. With each inhalation and exhalation, our breath revitalizes each cell, each nerve, each organ.

Meditative Breathing

The Chicago Zoological Society's Dolphin Connection at Hawk's Cay Resort is located in a sizable lagoon alongside the main canal for boats into and out of the Marina. Guests are offered daily dolphin programs and can also arrange to go down to the dock in the lagoon to meet the dolphins up close.

The "dolphin deck" is a shaded area of the resort's wide porch just above the dolphin lagoon. The relaxing atmosphere experienced by resort guests can only be accomplished by the hustling of resort staff, who take advantage of this peaceful spot as a favorite place to take a break, watch dolphins being dolphins, listen to their hypnotic breathing, and relax for a few minutes before returning to their jobs.

One of the more stressful positions at the resort is that of "Manager-On-Duty," the person who deals with any and all problems which may arise during a shift. One Manager-On-Duty commonly arrived early to spend time on the dolphin deck, relaxing and settling his mind before facing the guests and their problems.

Newly arrived guests were sometimes referred to the dolphin deck as a place to let go of the stress they'd brought with them and move into the peaceful rhythm of their surroundings. One frazzled guest had left her medication in her room and broken her key in the lock just minutes before she was scheduled to go out on a snorkel boat trip. The Manager-On-Duty was able to help, with a calm that amazed and impressed the frantic woman. He recommended she spend some time on the dolphin deck in the mornings, when only a few people were around, sit in a deck chair, take some slow, deep breaths, and watch and listen to the dolphins. "It's hard to explain the calming effect they have on people," he said, "but somehow they can put us into a different state of mind. You come away feeling both mellow and energized."

Dolphins are masters of the peace of silence. To listen to the quiet, rhythmic breathing of a pod of dolphins at night is to feel transported into the wordless harmony of their society.

The Power of Breath

The breath can be a source of great power—it is the key to aligning body, mind, and spirit. Therapeutic breath work can cure many ills, physical or emotional, as the mind follows the body. Check your breathing right now. Is it tense and shallow? Deep breathing is commonly taught as a vital part of relaxation techniques. Many forms of meditation use the breath as a means to enter the required state of physical relaxation leading to spiritual attunement. Some philosophies attach great meaning and symbolism to how we experience our breath. The yogis say if you can control your breath, you can control your life, and that he who only half breathes, half lives. Let your breath surround your movements. It is so simple, so basic, and can refresh all aspects of your being.

Part Four

HEART

IT IS IN THE REALM of the heart that many people encounter the essence of a dolphin. While it may be impossible to know for sure what a dolphin is feeling, during an encounter, people often receive strong impressions of the animal's mood, its personality, and its attitude toward them.

These impressions are not to be discounted just because they are not conveyed through the medium of words. Only a small percentage of our knowledge of other people is conveyed in words; we all know how difficult it can be to understand what someone else is feeling, or to adequately communicate what we are feeling to someone else. Certainly we can't count on words alone. Yet, we can understand much about a person by interpreting their actions, their facial expressions, their posture, their tone of voice, and the look in their eyes, as well as other indescribable some-things that tell us about a person's character and mood, and thus their heart and spirit.

An important element of our understanding of dolphins comes when we bring to bear faculties other than our intellects. Dolphins can teach us to exercise our empathy, our gentleness, our capacity for joy, and the freeing power of play to fully experience all life has to offer.

NURTURING

WHAT IS IT that makes us care for each other? What is it that makes a mother care for her child? Whatever it is, the quality of nurturing is shared throughout the animal kingdom. It is one of the more delightful qualities we can say we have in common with many animals, and notably with dolphins.

It is critical to the propagation of a mammalian species that an animal should take good care of its young. Many nurturing behaviors and feelings probably evolved due to this genetic imperative. A mammal gives birth to only a few precious offspring, sometimes just one or two at a time, and may spend years nursing and caring for

Above: Merina with her nursling Pandora at the Dolphin Research Center.

them before giving birth again. Each new little being represents a very great, long-term investment.

It seems that dolphins have built-in empathy—and so, too, do we. But to say that compassion is a genetic trait geared toward survival of the species takes nothing away from the concept. It is rather comforting to think that we are genetically wired for compassion and nurturing.

Nurturing, by definition, refers to physical nourishing as well as teaching, and fostering development. It includes all those activities that help a being to grow and develop, to thrive, to flourish. For humans, nurturing can mean a mother nursing her baby, a father teaching a child to play a game, a friend telling you it's time to take a break, a teacher giving individual attention to a student with a learning disability, or one spouse encouraging the other to pursue a dream.

Dolphin Care-Givers

As the time draws near for a mother dolphin to give birth, another experienced female, perhaps a sister or daughter, may attend her. This mid-wife dolphin will fend off unwanted interference from other dolphins, such as curious males, and help keep a look-out for predators. She may help to push the calf to the surface for that critical first breath, coming up under its soft belly and lifting it with her snout.

When dolphin calves are first born, they nurse frequently, in brief sessions, around the clock. As mammals, dolphin mothers nurse their young, which could be rather problematic as an underwater activity—can you imagine any other mammal managing it? Dolphins don't drink salt water; they get all their fluids from their food, metabolized from the cells of the fish they eat, or in the case of calves, from their mother's milk. In terms of the availability of fresh water, oceans are the greatest deserts on the planet. The back of a dolphin's throat is closed by a sphincter muscle that encircles it and helps keep the salt water out. When a dolphin is "sitting up" with an open mouth, you can sometimes see a little pool of water in the back of its throat.

Since the calves must be able to drink mother's milk without swallowing a lot of salt water, dolphins have a clever solution. A dolphin calf has no teeth in the very front of its inflexible mouth—there is a gap which accommodates the nipple that will protrude from one of the two mammary slits on a mother dolphin's lower abdomen. The baby dolphin will nuzzle against a mammary slit, and, as mom presents her nipple, roll its tongue around it. The edges of its tongue are fringed; the fringe is long when the calf is young, usually wearing down as it gets older. This fringe interlocks like a zipper when the calf rolls its tongue into a tube, and mom can pump milk through this tube without the salt water getting in. Nursing in this fashion, it only takes a few seconds for the calf to get a good dose of the mother dolphin's very rich, fatty milk.

Incredibly, instances of spontaneous lactation have taken place among dolphins. At one facility, when a still-nursing calf's mother became ill, another dolphin in the group, with no calf of her own to nurse, and not even pregnant, began to produce milk and took over nursing the calf in need. In the wild, a previously dry female was seen taking over the nursing of an orphaned calf.

A young dolphin calf stays very close to its mother, swimming in an echelon position beside her. In this position, the calf does not have to swim as strongly as the adults; rather, it is drafted along in the mother's slipstream and so is able to keep up with the pod. This position is also convenient for nursing. A mother dolphin stays in close physical contact with her calf, steering it with her body and using her pectoral fins and rostrum to interact with it. She may sometimes lift a boisterous calf on her back or rostrum, effectively stranding the rowdy youngster and keeping it under control.

Bee was the quintessential dolphin mother of the Dolphin Research Center. Not only did she raise three fat and sassy daughters of her own, but Bee extended her vast capacity for nurturing to other species as well. Dart was a spotted dolphin who was found by fishermen in the Lower Keys, a tiny calf stranded all alone in the shallows. Although no spotted dolphin had ever survived a stranding before, and Dart's young age hurt her chances even further, she was brought to the Dolphin Research Center where staff dedicated themselves to giving Dart a fighting chance.

At first, the little dolphin was quarantined in a separate lagoon. Bee could see the calf from her area and, although she was nursing her own calf, Omega, Bee seemed desperately interested in Dart. Staff thought it safest for Dart to remain apart, but she continued to pine away. Finally, there seemed nothing to lose, and gates were dropped to allow Bee into Dart's area. Bee lost no time in swimming to Dart and rounding her up as she would a calf of her own. Bee adopted this different species, raised her along with Omega, and taught the other dolphins to treat her gently.

Mom Can't Do It Alone

Dolphins have a close-knit society. Adult dolphins exhibit nurturing behavior when they support a struggling member of their pod, and a great deal of time and effort is spent in the care and training of young dolphins, from the time they are born, and for many years afterward.

As her calf grows, a wild dolphin mother still has to keep up with the pod, and get enough to eat—a nursing mother is eating for two. (Facilities that care for dolphins have been able to observe and record a great deal of important information about dolphins' needs and habits, and records show that a nursing mother may eat twice as much fish as she would ordinarily.) Other dolphins, usually adult females, will take on baby-sitting duties, swimming with the calf in tow to give the mother a break and a chance to hunt and feed.

The mother may keep the calf with her and demonstrate hunting techniques as she forages. She will catch fish and give them to the calf, who starts eating some fish when it's a few months old, although it is still reliant on nursing for most of its nutrition. A bottlenose dolphin calf will eat more and more fish and nurse less and less for two or more years, depending on the robustness of the calf and, judging by behavior observed in captive dolphins, the mother's personality. Some mothers keep their calves close to them as long as possible; some allow the youngsters much more freedom at an earlier age, and these calves are probably weaned sooner.

From Susan Barco, Research Scientist, Virginia Marine Science Museum:

Often when we're observing a big mixed group of mothers and calves that probably includes some older calves and juveniles, it seems that the juveniles run interference. They come around the boat while the moms sneak away with the young calves. They are very protective of their kids.

There is much to learn about living in a dolphin's complex society, and dolphin calves learn by mimicking their elders. Perhaps because of the flexibility of their society, many dolphins participate in helping the youngsters to flourish. Adult females will start teaching even young calves about sexuality by rubbing and caressing and swimming belly to belly. Adult male spotted dolphins in the Bahamas have been observed engaging in what looks like mock fighting with young males of only two or three years of age. Young dolphins at about three to five years old begin to spend time together in juvenile pods, where they practice grown-up games, but can rejoin the main group if they feel threatened.

Caring for Humans

Wild dolphins have been credited for thousands of years with helping to protect people in trouble at sea. For many people, one of the most endearing dolphin traits is that their empathy seems to extend to other species, including us, as evidenced in the following story:

It was a Wednesday morning snorkeling trip to the Looe Key coral reefs in the Florida Keys National Marine Sanctuary in 1992. Participants did not know if they would get a chance to snorkel because the weather had been rough for over a week, seas were high and underwater visibility limited.

About half-way out on the three-mile trip, the first mate spotted something floating low on the water's surface quite a distance away. It soon became apparent they were coming upon a raft of Cuban refugees trying to reach Florida. As the boat got a little closer, the entire crew could see three dolphins swimming in a wide circle around the raft. As it turned out, seven people had strapped together two wooden pallets and attached these pallets to inner tubes, and then cast their fates to the winds and currents. As soon as the snorkel boat got near the Cuban refugees, the dolphins disappeared.

One of the people aboard the snorkel boat spoke fluent Spanish and was able to converse with the refugees when the boat got alongside. Through translation, the Captain learned to his astonishment that this was their eighth day since leaving Cuba in the dark of night with only the clothes on their backs and a few supplies. He could not comprehend what they must have endured because seas had been at twelve to sixteen feet for the past several days out in the gulf stream. How they had survived those rough seas in their homemade flotation device was a miracle. They were totally out of food and water, badly sunburned with blistered lips, and the salt spray encrusting their faces had given them a ghostly appearance.

The refugees said they had been OK for the first day or so, but by the third day the weather turned and they had been saying their final prayers, fully expecting to be lost at sea. At their lowest moment, the three dolphins appeared and began slowly circling their raft. As soon as they saw the dolphins, they knew they would make it to Florida. The dolphins were considered "good luck," offering protection and, more importantly, giving hope to desperate people. The escort stayed with them for five more days until encountering the snorkel boat.

Within an hour, a Coast Guard vessel arrived and took the refugees safely aboard. They were only sorry they couldn't somehow thank the three dolphins who, as far as they were concerned, had saved their lives.

Now that dolphins have been brought into close contact with people in facilities, we often can see how effective their powers of nurturing are.

From Jane Fink, Tierra Verde, Florida:

Formerly, I worked with the Dolphin/Child therapy program at the Dolphin Research Center. The children participating had a variety of physical limitations that restricted or directed the type of interaction they might have with the dolphins. Without fail, the dolphins adapted to these special needs without any direction from the staff.

For example, when giving a dorsal pull during a public swim session, if an able bodied swimmer released his or her hold on the dorsal fin, the dolphin would return to the trainer at the dock. The "ride" was over. However, on many occasions in the therapy program when children were unable to maintain a grip on the dorsal fin due to such problems as cerebral palsy, the dolphins would stop and wait for the child to grab hold again and then adjust their speed and pull according to the intensity of the grip.

Dolphin/child therapy program participant gets a gentle dorsal pull.

One child, Scott, could only use one finger to grip the dorsal fin. There was no way that he could hold onto the dolphin during a pull, or so we thought. When he put his finger over A.J.'s dorsal fin and A.J. started to move, Scott immediately lost his grip. A.J. promptly stopped, backed up, and let Scott try again. After a second attempt failed, A.J. repeated his back-up maneuver and, this time, pulled so slowly that Scott was able to maintain his grip. This is something no one had tried to teach A.J. He evaluated the situation and adjusted his behavior accordingly.

Sometimes, dolphins will look out for able-bodied swimmers, no matter that they are of a different species, and not part of their "family." One participant in the swim program at the Dolphin Research Center was having the time of his life, laughing continuously as the dolphin mimicked his every move, shook "hands" with him, gently kissed him on the cheek, and used its snout to push him by the feet in a wide circle as he floated on his back. Near the end of the swim, the man swam as fast as he could, looking underwater through his snorkel mask at the intriguing eye of the dolphin swimming right next to him. He had only gone a few yards in this manner when another dolphin suddenly swam right in front of him, blocking his way. The man popped to the surface, pulled back his mask onto the top of his head, and asked the trainer on the dock, "What was that all about?"

The trainer pointed out, "Well, that was Omega, and she just prevented you from swimming right into that wall of coral just ahead of you. She didn't want to see you hurt yourself and probably figured the best way to stop you was to just plant herself so you couldn't go any further."

Opening Your Heart

The farther we extend our nurturing, the richer our lives will be. We are sometimes so stingy with our caring; we only extend it to those whom we believe to be like us. The time has come to extend ourselves beyond the notion that we are the most important, whether the "we" is a village, a nation, or a species. To whom does your nurturing extend? Immediate family? Friends? Strangers? Co-workers? Your community? Other animals? Other races? Those in need worldwide? There are many opportunities to tap into the wealth of goodness in the world. It begins when you share the goodness within you.

Begin by nurturing yourself, so that your personal well of self-esteem and love will be full. You cannot take care of someone else if you are physically, mentally, emotionally, or spiritually exhausted. Don't be afraid to ask for what you need. Then, be willing to nurture those around you, remembering that sometimes the ones who need it most are the most grumpy or aloof. Be generous in your nurturing; there are so many people out there who need your love and care. Even if they are strangers to you, you can quickly bridge the gap by believing that we are all connected at the level of heart and spirit. In this practice of cherishing other living beings may lie our best hope for learning to live in harmony with the Earth.

PLAY

DOLPHINS ARE NATURALLY athletic, vigorous, playful animals. Wild dolphins find playthings, like seaweed or rocks, in their natural habitat. Active behavior, like leaps and high dives out of the water, at least sometimes seem to be done for the pure joy of it—because they can. Not only do the youngsters play, but playfulness is found in old and young, male and female. Dolphin play involves a great amount of physical contact and has important social content as youngsters learn appropriate forms of interaction with their peers and their elders, and adults renew social contacts as they come and go between sub-pods.

Above: A.J., Talon, Tursi, and Theresa reach for the sky at the Dolphin Research Center.

Dolphin Games

Dolphins sometimes are willing to include humans in their games. When Major joined a research project in the Bahamas, he had several opportunities to interact with wild spotted dolphins in their watery world. His journal tells the story:

I don't know what words to use to express the feelings of being eye-to-eye with dolphins, body-to-body, twisting, diving, spinning, playing games, watching a mother teaching her calf to catch fish, being playful, trusting and totally unconditional. When the thirty-minute encounter ended, the games didn't. Captain Dan fired up the Stenella and all ten dolphins rode the bow wave for fifteen minutes. It was as if this was our gift to them for coming in to be with us, and they seemed to enjoy it immensely.

Keep in mind that dolphins do not live in a stress-free world. Like any wild animal, they must constantly find enough of the right kind of food, avoid predators, and protect their young. Marine animals must also avoid boat traffic and fishing nets, and fight the effects of pollution on their environment. Sadly, even in the beautiful, clear blue waters of the Bahamas, there is floating garbage and marine debris to be seen. Yet, dolphins teach us to revel in the moment, to lighten up, to laugh and play whenever we can.

From Mary Ann Little, teacher, Sebring, Florida:

For me, the greatest life lessons are in the playing. The dolphins get and give such joy and amusement in the simplest of games. It doesn't matter what you're wearing, and they don't particularly care if you start out in a bad mood! They are a wonderful reminder that in playing together there is friendship and connection.

Dolphins in human care demonstrate delightful creativity in the games they invent. They approach new situations with wide-eyed curiosity and exuberance—if it's possible to make a game of it, they will. Dolphins connect with life through active participation—like children, this is how they learn about their world. They are naturally imitative and delight in mimicking sounds and actions of other animals and people. Wild dolphins, too, include mimicking games in their interactions with swimmers. We are never sure if they are honoring us, learning about us, or just making fun of us!

From Major's journal, Bahamas, July 5, 1994:

Billy had three dolphins with him constantly and had the most fun diving head first to the bottom, about twenty feet down, remaining upside down while the three mimicked and circled around him.

Trainers are always looking for new games to try—a favorite of the dolphins is when a trainer paddles across the pool on a surfboard. Some can pick up enough speed that the dolphins surf alongside, or sometimes the dolphins offer a tow. They've even been known to leap completely over trainer and board in a graceful arc.

A Sense of Humor

Do dolphins have a sense of humor? Former trainer Cori Trudeau (now an Interpretive Naturalist at the Minnesota Zoo) has this story to tell about a dolphin practical joker:

I have spent a great deal of time thinking about dolphins, trying to decide what it is about them that intrigues, inspires, and fascinates me. Of course, it's the whole package; they are wise and playful, beautiful and graceful, but what I love best about them is their sense of humor. Very few animals I have worked with have the sense of humor of a dolphin. It always came through during those moments between training sessions, when I wasn't trying to "control" the action.

Early in my dolphin training career, I worked with an older dolphin named Connie. Connie was in her late twenties and had been around the block a few times. She had a reputation for breaching (jumping up in the air and coming down on her side) with precision timing, soaking unsuspecting people who were walking by her pool. What was in it for her? Watching people run screaming as a sheet of water soaked them! It must have been quite entertaining because she did it every chance she got.

One summer evening, a couple of other trainers and I were leaving for home.
Each night we let all eight Atlantic bottlenose dolphins into the main pool together.
It had glass sides about eight feet tall all around the front. We were walking along-
side the glass, watching the dolphins play. When I reached the far side, I noticed
Connie was sitting near the bottom of the pool, facing out, looking directly at me.
This seemed a bit odd so I moved in closer to get a better look at her. Her lure was
working. As I got close to the side, Connie slowly rose to the surface. I looked up
through the side to try and see what she was doing. That's when Connie dumped
what felt like a bucketful, but was really a mouthful, of water on my head. She then
slowly lowered herself back down, still facing me and just stared. If dolphins can
laugh, she was doing it! This was my first exposure to dolphin fun, and although
she had duped me good, I was absolutely amazed by the experience.

Dolphin Research Center staff members who have been tied to their desks for too
long are encouraged to schedule dock time with the dolphins—just to be around
them, listen to their measured breathing, watch their antics, soak up some sun, and,
if the dolphins are in the mood, give them back rubs—stroking their smooth skin
as they offer a broad gray back, or flipper, for your touch—or join their games, toss-
ing seaweed again and again, catching it or ducking as it is tossed back to you.
Dolphins are spontaneous and seemingly love to joke. Stories of the dolphins' games
fill Susie's journal:

I was hurrying by the front lagoon on an errand to another building only to be stopped in my tracks as a wet wad of seaweed splatted against my leg. I had been pelted once again by a dolphin, and looked over to see three gray faces bobbing in the water, eyes twinkling with an invitation to come down onto the floating docks and play. Yesterday, Aleta got me with a mangrove pod that she tossed all the way over the boardwalk as I was leaving her pool after dock time. She knows she's irresistible.

It's hard to be tense and worried if you're chortling with glee as you engage in a splashing game with a dolphin.

Everybody Needs Play

Why is play important, and what does this mean to you in your work-a-day world? It's simple—play keeps you open. In our society, we are taught to "act like grown-ups," to get serious, to leave playfulness behind in childhood. If you've forgotten how to be playful, you may need extra help (such as being around a puppy, or a child—or a dolphin) before you can be comfortably uninhibited and bring play back to your daily life.

The Dolphin Research Center's structured swim program attracts people from all over the world who come for the privilege of spending time in the water with bottlenose dolphins. They spend a half-day at the Center, learning about dolphins and conservation issues, and receiving instruction in what to expect and how to behave during their swim.

All kinds of people enroll in this program. Occasionally, you see the tough dad or boyfriend who swears he is only there because of the kids, wife, or girlfriend—like one gruff fellow who arrived with his wife saying, "This is *her* idea of fun." He may have started out with a detached attitude, but once he got in the water with the dolphins, it only took a few seconds. The macho attitude fell away, and he became a kid again, smiling, laughing, and yelling as he was pulled through the water holding on to a dorsal fin. When the swim was over, he was bubbly and teary-eyed and couldn't stop talking about the incredible experience of being eye-to-eye with a five hundred-pound creature who treated him as gingerly as a baby. He couldn't wait to see the photos his wife took of him being kissed by one of the dolphins!

Jayne Shannon, President and General Manager at the Dolphin Research Center, and mother of three, compares working with dolphins to being with children. "Dolphins have that incredible thirst for new things, exciting things, fun things," says Jayne. Children and dolphins spontaneously and honestly interact with others who touch their lives, inevitably spreading laughter in their paths. "Dolphins teach you to laugh at yourself," says Jayne. "You have to be ready to be flexible."

You can't be open to new ideas if your mind is weary and over-crowded. You can't be open to the people around you and build successful and satisfying relationships if you are so tense your neck aches and your stomach is in knots. Play relaxes you, clears your brain, and refreshes your body, which, as ample evidence proves, is necessary for good health and peak functioning.

If you want your creativity to flow—approach that project as play. If you want to teach—make a game of it. If you want to loosen up a group of people—get them laughing, get them moving, get them to play together. A non-threatening environment brings out the best in everyone. When you are relaxed and smiling, you let go of your fear, and you can learn a lot about yourself and others, without even trying.

Like the dolphins, lighten up and revel in the moment.

JOY

J OY IS AN ELUSIVE CONCEPT. Like love, most of us would say we know what it is, or have ideas about it, but our attempts to define it somehow fall short of the truth of the experience. Joy is not so much something to be learned or defined, as something to recognize. Whatever joy is, apparently human beings both desire it and have access to it.

It's easy to connect joy and dolphins for many reasons. Joy is like the water that is the dolphin's home—it flows, it rushes, it bursts through to the surface, it ebbs, it is a quiet pool in the center of being. Our experience of joy reflects the colors and

Above: Pure joy—Susie with Merina and Aleta.

light of our minds and spirits. Its existence is universally known, the truth of it universally felt, the possibility of it universally desired.

We often experience joy as an unleashing of something that was there all along. Once we leave childhood behind, we sometimes get out of touch with the well of our joy. Watch a baby of any kind—whether it be a human child, a puppy, kitten, colt, or a dolphin calf—and you are reminded. The exuberance of a young animal is the joy of being alive, full of health and innocence, bursting with potential.

Joy, like dolphins, may be quiet or boisterous, but it is powerful and life-affirming. Joy can underlie sad times, giving support and grounding in the knowledge that you are loved even when other things in your life may be going wrong, or in the understanding that you have the potential to be joyful because you are alive. Sometimes joy is sharpest in contrast to tragedy, as though the darkness makes the light glow all the brighter.

Being around dolphins seems to open our potential for joy. Time and time again this has been expressed by visitors to the Dolphin Research Center.

The Inner Light

Lindley was a bright young man trapped in a wheelchair, his body in the grip of cerebral palsy. He could not control his arms and legs, and his hands were cruelly bent. With the help of his parents, and DRC staff members, Lindley donned a life jacket and entered the dolphins' watery world. Lindley worked with a young male dolphin named A.J. Throughout the session, those present were touched by the little dolphin's gentleness. A.J. just waited patiently while Lindley leaned his head against the dolphin's side, breathing hard, practicing relaxation techniques in an effort to be able to open his hand enough to grasp A.J.'s dorsal fin. Finally, A.J. moved off slowly with Lindley holding on. Lindley's smile radiated the joy and triumph that moment held for him.

The radiance of joy released—Lindley and his father with A.J.

What is the role of the dolphin in this story? The dolphin is the focus of Lindley's effort, of his desire, and that is what brought about the joy and triumph. The accomplishment belonged to Lindley, and the family, friends, and therapists who had brought him thus far. A.J.'s behavior may seem atypical of a dolphin, an animal that we usually see as so very active and energetic. Yet, time and again, dolphins in interaction with humans demonstrate the capability for patience, gentleness, and adaptability, for reading a situation and the needs of a special individual. The dolphin supplied unconditional love and acceptance—the magic that released the joy in Lindley as well as in his mother and father, and indeed, everyone present.

We have seen the bright light of joy in the faces of so many children and adults participating in dolphin-human therapy sessions. Smiles and childlike delight are seen in people of all ages when they are with dolphins. The interaction is experienced as a blessing, or a thrill, or a privilege. It is the same with people who have been working with dolphins for years, who have gotten to know individual dolphins and their personalities. The interaction may become familiar, but it is a deepening joy. And like love, the experience of joy inspires a certain gratitude—it makes you want to give back, to desire the most good for that which inspired the feeling.

Sharing the Joy

A young California woman named Melissa took a week's vacation to travel with a small group to San Ignacio, half way down the Baja Peninsula in Mexico, to witness the annual gray whale migration in February. Their guides were local fishermen who knew the waters and the whales well. The experience was overwhelming. It was a magical time when everyone was happy and no one gave any thought to their normal, busy world.

When she returned to work the following week, Melissa greatly missed the joy she had felt being among the whales, especially the mothers and calves, and was saddened to be back in her regular environment of freeways, office buildings, and rush, rush, rush. She felt depressed at work and only wished to be back among the whales.

Disillusioned and searching for answers, the next year she attended the Dolphin Research Center's Dolphinlab, a week-long educational experience during which students immerse themselves in the world of dolphins and learn about dolphin physiology, maternity, training, husbandry, communication, research, marine mammal law, and conservation of marine mammals and the environment. On the first night, when everyone was asked to express why they were there and what they hoped to learn from the week, Melissa said she wanted to discover what she could do differently so that when she returned to work this time she wouldn't get so depressed about being away from the wonderful experience of being close to marine mammals.

On the last night of Dolphinlab, when everyone described what the week had meant to them, Melissa cried with happiness as she told the group she had finally come to understand the message the dolphins and whales had been sending her. All she needed to do was carry that feeling of joy and unconditional love back with her and share it in everything she did—at work, at home, among family and friends. Melissa told everyone there to become a dolphin or whale in their own minds, which to her meant not trying to be anything else but what you are at the moment. "Live in the moment," she said. "Just be."

How do we stay in touch with our underpinnings, our potential for joy? Make a joyful noise. Play. Smile and laugh every chance you get. Smile now, as you are reading this. If you tend to be depressed or anxious, it may take practice, but there's nothing like repetition to instill new habits. Seek out things that make you smile, that bring you joy. Let go of people, places, and things that don't. Recall experiences that brought you joy, and feed off them. A dolphin will seek out ways to have fun and enjoy life—you can, too. Don't put off joy. It's accessible now. Taste the essences, hear the music, watch the colors radiate. Find and follow a spiritual practice that brings you joy. Bring joy into your daily life, and your presence will bring joy to others.

Part Five

SPIRIT

SOMETHING HAPPENS to people when their lives are touched by a dolphin. It is as though a mingling of dolphin and human spirits occurs, transcending the barriers of language, experience, environment, and reason. It is magic, and those involved experience a feeling of wonder and privilege.

Our stories reflect the spirit of a dolphin as seen through the eyes and hearts of humans. Understanding the powerful effect dolphins have on us may tell us something about dolphins, but can reveal much more about ourselves.

DEATH

Most of the time, to be around dolphins is to experience the many joys of life. But there are times when death prevails. The death of a dolphin you have known is heartbreaking, and even for those who deal professionally with stranded marine animals, the spectre of death may be strongly felt.

An animal that dies at sea will sometimes wash up on the beach, the margin between our worlds. The body joins the rest of the sea's offerings, animal, vegetable, and mineral—sand, shells, bits of a lady crab's body, a fish skeleton fought over by gulls, the tail from a horseshoe crab, skate egg cases that look like little horned

Above: Little Bit died as she had lived, on her own terms.

pouches, seaweed, piles of sea grass stems like haystacks of miniature bamboo along the tide line.

There will be something larger, something the unsuspecting observer perhaps can't, at first, identify. As the observer gets closer, the body becomes recognizable by sight—and, no doubt, by smell. Sadness is tempered by the intense interest of seeing the elusive animal up close. When a dolphin or whale is sighted at sea it is in motion and at least partially obscured by the water. When death comes and it strands, its body is a gift to study and learn from.

From Susie's journal, April, 1991:

It is lying belly up on the beach, flukes melting into the sand as the shallow tide waters recede, a beautiful, large dead body. Male pilot whale. About twelve feet long. Incredible, to touch an animal usually only glimpsed in motion, hidden in the sea. To see the strange V-shaped indentation on his forehead, characteristic of these odd members of the dolphin family. To look into his mouth, and see how the teeth grow. I'm fascinated by the colors and shapes and lines of this animal. He is so smooth, so elegant.

Maybe I should feel worse about the fact that he is dead, but I don't feel any keen sadness. It would be different, has been different, when there is evidence that the death was caused by human activity—propeller cuts, tell-tale impressions from rope, entanglement in monofilament line—or when it is an animal I know personally, have seen living, have interacted with, creature to creature. The life of the animal is removed from this body. I never knew him as an individual, to me he is a representative. I feel awe at the life processes that formed him.

So much of what I teach is an abstraction, learned from the written word. To touch the reality of this animal is astounding, delightful. So much to learn, so many questions. Everything about him is geared toward a life underwater—the stream-lined shape, the smooth skin, the elegant tail fluke, the fins instead of more famil-iar appendages, like arms, legs, hands, feet. I know all about the adaptations of marine mammals to their fluid environment, but now the physical reality is brought home to me—I know he's dead, but he looks so…uncomfortable…lying on the beach. So out of place. I long to see him floating.

The eye that's visible is closed—almost. It's open just a slit, enough that I can see the bright sunlight entering and shimmering in the reflective surfaces. I wonder how old he is, where he has been, what he has seen and felt. Then the sadness begins to come, the sense of loss that the individual is no more.

A network of volunteer teams around the country works to respond to stranded marine animals, gathering critical data. Often, a stranding refers to a dead animal washed ashore. Besides recording measurements and statistics such as where and when an animal strands, a necropsy (or post-mortem operation) may be performed to collect tissue samples and see what can be determined about the causes of death.

Susan Barco, a Research Scientist at the Virginia Marine Science Museum, has performed many post-mortem examinations on stranded dolphins:

No matter how sad the death of a dolphin, it gives us a rare opportunity to get close to one. You can't really know dolphins until you have examined them from the inside out. It gives us a whole other level of understanding. I have never appreciated an animal more than when I looked inside it. That's the only way to realize how amazingly well adapted dolphins are to their environment. You can't fully understand how they live until you have examined them in death.

But a stranded dolphin or whale is not always dead. Then the story becomes one of rapid mobilization of teams, great effort, resources solicited and exhausted, weary hours, a battle waged and usually lost, with an occasional comforting victory when an animal can be rehabilitated and returned to the sea. A stranded dolphin provides an opportunity to try medical procedures, to identify viruses or other diseases that may be affecting a wild population, to observe, to theorize, to learn.

For the volunteer, standing in the water with arms around a live dolphin, supporting it in the absence of its pod, it's an opportunity to feel close, to try to provide nurturing and comfort, to try to communicate without words.

From Susie's journal, April 1992:

It's late at night, and I've been standing for hours waist deep in the water supporting this dolphin, this living being so different from myself. Does she know how

I feel? Does she understand that we are trying to help? Or is she just weak and too sick to care? I try, illogically, to send her my thoughts, and to read her mind. I wish I could do a mind meld to know once and for all what a dolphin's thoughts are like. I don't think she is frightened of us, but I don't know for sure. She seems mostly to be turned inward, and I hope her inward focus means she is healing, like a dog or cat that shuts down because all its energy is being used to accomplish the most immediate need.

Accepting Death

All animals avoid death, presumably because the strongest of genetic prerogatives is to hold on to life. If it's sick or injured, an animal does what it can to conserve energy and heal. If it's in danger, it shows fear, and acts to preserve itself and (sometimes) its comrades. We don't know if any of the human preoccupation with death is felt in the animal world. It is interesting to note that dolphins have been recorded sounding the signature whistles of dead comrades long after those dolphins are gone. Are they remembering them? Looking for them? Talking about them? We do not know.

It has been reported that dolphins sharing a pool with an ailing dolphin may react to their poolmate's death as though nothing were different—continuing their daily routines despite the body lying on the bottom of the pool. It's as though, once the living dolphins determine that their mate is dead, they are truly able to let go, exhibiting an emotional resilience we often lack.

This is the case at the Dolphin Research Center when a dolphin dies—the humans are numbed by grief, while the dolphins seem to bounce back immediately. Bee had been ill for weeks. As her strength failed, she was not deserted by her daughters, Merina and Omega, and her adopted daughter, Dart, the spotted dolphin. They flanked her, stayed with her, and supported her as she grew weaker and more emaciated in her final days. Staff watched in amazement as little Omega, only two years old, swam underneath Bee, holding her up and guiding her around for hours. Bee died in the early morning, her body slipping peacefully below the surface. Only Omega, who turned out to have still been nursing, seemed shaken. As is so often the case, the surviving dolphins ignored the body as an empty shell, and life went on as usual.

An exception to this scenario seems to be the case of a mother losing a calf. Then the mother will sometimes push the body around for days, almost as though trying to wake up the dead little one. No acceptance of death is evident at that point. Finally, perhaps because the decomposing corpse ceases to bear much resemblance to a living calf, the mother will give it up. Sometimes a mother dolphin will appear to mourn the loss of a calf—she won't eat, won't associate with people or even other dolphins for a time. The bond between mother and child is nature's most powerful, and one not easily broken.

Unfortunately, the worst threats faced by wild dolphins are directly or indirectly related to people: dolphins die in gill nets, drift nets, purse-seine nets, and ghost nets; become entangled in or ingest marine debris, which when swallowed can cause internal injury or clog their digestive tracts so they starve; are affected by loss of habitat and over-fishing, which can make it difficult to find food; are stressed by the ever-increasing noise pollution we pour into their habitat; and are weakened by pollution in the form of toxins that can taint their food and lead to immune system suppression and reproductive failure (including still-born calves).

From Captain Iain Kerr, Whale Conservation Institute, Lincoln, Massachusetts:

If you look at any species of animal, you see that animals adapt to nature. Humans adapt nature to suit themselves. And we've created compounds to which nature has no antidotes. We're dumping things like PCBs in the ocean, that dissolve in fat, not water. They bio-amplify up the foodchain, and produce the "generation effect," where the marine mammal mother, in her milk, passes along 30 percent of her toxic debt to the next generation.

Aside from people-related dangers, dolphins' worst enemies are disease, predators, and parasites. A dolphin calf has a greater chance of succumbing to any of those dangers than an older dolphin. Like other mammals, the first two years of life are often the most critical.

Do dolphins know when they are going to die? It's impossible to know what goes through their minds, or what concept of death they may have, but they could have the same sense that causes a dog or cat to crawl off into a secluded place to die.

Certainly dolphins avoid death with great energy; one could say all their energy is directed toward an avoidance of death. Finding food, bearing young to perpetuate the species, protecting themselves against predators—these are all ways of staying alive. It is not on death that they dwell. They simply go about the business of life.

For many years, Lynne Calero was Medical Director at the Dolphin Research Center. She considers the death of Little Bit, who was believed to be over forty years old when she died, to be one of the most marvelous things she's ever had the privilege of witnessing:

Little Bit died exactly as she had lived—in total control and on her own terms. She'd had a serious infection we'd been struggling with for two weeks. I haven't had many clear-cut intuitive blasts from dolphins, but I'd just been with Little Bit when I suddenly knew she was getting ready to die. I walked back to the office and told the staff they'd better say their goodbyes.

Jayne [Shannon, President and General Manager of DRC] had just walked down to the lagoon when Little Bit beached herself, struggling to breathe. Jayne jumped down to the little beach, and pulled Little Bit upright, holding this big dolphin in her arms, and calling for me and Linda [Erb, Director of Animal Care and Training]. We supported her blowhole above water and as soon as she could breathe, Little Bit looked at us, got totally peaceful, and died. I really think Little Bit wanted certain people there. She didn't want to drown; she wanted people around to help. She got it all organized. When Jayne asked how I had known, I said, "She told me. I followed Little Bit's orders, just like I always have." Then we all just started laughing and crying and swapping stories.

We are often embarrassed by grief and especially avoid talk of death. A person who is dying has difficulty finding someone with whom to discuss his or her feelings. Most people say, "Don't talk like that, you're going to be fine," whether it's true or not. Sometimes people need for you to be there, not to solve their problems or offer advice, but just to be there for them. Dolphins (or people) supporting a dying member of their pod cannot save that dolphin's life. They are simply there, offering support, keeping it afloat so it does not have to drown or die alone. We don't know when death will come; we can only accept it as a natural part of life.

Death provides us the great gift of unity with all living things. No matter how vast our differences appear while we live, there is solidarity among all of earth's inhabitants in our dying.

TRUST & ACCEPTANCE

NOT MANY WILD animals offer us a chance to relate to them the way bottlenose and spotted dolphins do. Dolphins seem approachable; they offer us a way to connect with the joy and freedom of close attunement with the natural world. The honor of being accepted by a dolphin somehow makes us feel good about ourselves. We forget about our feelings of separation and loneliness.

From Melissa DeVaughn, Outdoor Writer, Eagle River, Alaska:
There's something about a dolphin's eyes that makes me feel at ease, as if I'm with an old friend, a confidant, someone who will always make sure I'm

Above: The most important element in this relationship is trust. Trainer Shelley Samm at the Dolphin Research Center.

safe. I don't think of them as "animals," although the scientist in me tells me I should. Instead, I prefer to think of them as the representation of all that is free, honest, and good. I have no explanation for these feelings—they are as much a part of me as waking up, loving my husband, or nurturing my child. It is only natural, as it should be.

Accepting Our Help

While many species of dolphin are elusive, the ones with which we are most familiar, notably bottlenose and spotted dolphins, have often exhibited trust and a lack of fear in our presence. Sometimes, even the less familiar species we see only in a stranding situation (in this case, false killer whales, which, like orcas, are members of the diverse dolphin family) behave with a similar acceptance:

From Lynne Calero, Medical Director, Northeast Marine Animal Lifeline, Saco, Maine:

Time and time again, I have seen cetaceans [dolphins, whales, and porpoises], whether in the wild or in human care, demonstrate what seems to be insight into our intentions toward them, even in emergency situations. For example, in the middle 1980s a large group of more than twenty false killer whales stranded in the Key West area. They were being shepherded into a boat basin in an attempt to assess their condition. A group of four adults and one newborn was the first to arrive. The little one got stuck under part of an overhanging dock and was unable to surface to breathe. The concept of something over your head is certainly alien to this deep ocean species.

A crowd of people was there with me, but no one I knew or trusted. The adult whales were all shoving the baby with increasing panic in a futile attempt to free her. I had a split second to decide between two choices. I could sit and watch as this baby most likely drowned, or I could get in the water with no guarantee that anyone there would help me should these eight-hundred-pound, sometimes-carnivorous whales not want me near the calf. I got in.

I had to climb over the backs of two of them and step in front of the third to reach the calf. All of the whales were calm, allowing me to grasp the baby and pull her out. They never flinched as I climbed back over them, even though some were so badly sunburned that their muscle layer was exposed. I know of no other group of creatures on earth who would allow another species to handle one of their young in an emergency situation, especially while they were physically suffering as well. It is my personal belief that cetaceans have the ability to interpret our actions and deliberately choose to cooperate with and trust us. I wish people as a group did that well with each other.

In the years that Captain Wayne "Scott" Smith has spent with wild Atlantic spotted dolphins in the Little Bahama Bank, he has built a unique relationship with these dolphins and knows many of them as individuals. The following incredible story reflects the kind of inner-species bond that is possible between humans and dolphins.

From "Dolphin Tales" by W. Scott Smith with B.L. Bruigom:

In 1987, I began having a great deal of contact with a young female dolphin named Notcho. Although she was one of the dolphins that never liked to be touched, Notcho was extremely animated and loved to swim and play for hours at my side. I missed her greatly when, in 1990 and 1991, she became sexually active, stopped looking for human attention, and would only swim with and court the male dolphins. Early in 1992, I realized that she had become pregnant. As we finished our final trip for that season in October, I last saw Notcho looking very pregnant.

I was curious all winter, wondering what had happened to Notcho. Did she have a healthy baby? What would she be like now? Finally, in March of 1993, when I couldn't stand the suspense any longer, I took the boat over to the Bahamas to search for her.

Wayne "Scott" Smith, The Dolphin Dream Team

Notcho and her first born daughter Hali.

I spent the first day finding every dolphin, it seemed, except Notcho. I admit, I was worried about her. But by the second day, my worries were laid to rest. I found Notcho very far north and she instantly recognized the sound of the engines. I jumped in the water and it was just as it had been before she became sexually active.

The baby (I named her Hali) kept peeking from around Notcho. First she would look under her. Then she would pop her head over the top. It was apparent I was the first human Hali had ever seen. The more Notcho would play with me, the more comfortable Hali became. It didn't take long for her to put herself between Notcho and me.

After playing for some time, the most remarkable thing happened. Notcho, the nursing mother, took off to feed, leaving me to baby-sit Hali. Unbelievable! I had often seen mothers baby-sit for each other, but here I was, Scott, baby-sitting. I was honored and amazed! The trust that Notcho put in me still takes my breath away. Notcho was gone for close to half an hour. When she returned we continued to play for a while longer, and, eventually, they took off.

I sat on board the Dream Too *and watched them swim away. I was completely overwhelmed by this incredible experience.*

Accepting Diversity

It would seem dolphins have much to teach us about acceptance and trust of those who are different from ourselves. We are so quick to label others as friend or enemy. Spending time, sharing experiences and learning to understand them often negate our initial feelings of distrust or dislike of people we think are "different."

This is also true of our attitudes toward the animal kingdom.

From Teresa Winter, author and licensed therapist, Saco, Maine:

There is nothing like the first encounter with a dolphin in the wild. It is an unexpected delight to be with something this special. How comfortable I have become with jumping off the side of a boat into the water because the call of dolphins goes out. How quickly I ignore the fact we saw a large tiger shark in these same waters just yesterday. How quickly, I notice, my mind wants to label the dolphins good and the shark bad when, in fact, they are both parts of nature—the yin and the yang of it. The shark has as much right to be here as the dolphins; he (or she) also has a story to tell.

Every being has a unique inner nature. Together, we form the marvelous web of life. In each of us is something special, and we need to first accept and trust our own inner nature, and then accept and, indeed, celebrate, what is special and different about each other.

The practice of acceptance paves the way to a balanced view of others. Acknowledging and appreciating our sameness brings peace and unity. Respecting and enjoying our differences enriches our lives by broadening our perspective, awakening our minds, and opening our hearts.

BEYOND WORDS

IT IS DIFFICULT TO describe adequately the effect that interactions with dolphins have on people. The opening of the heart, empowerment, suspension of time, release of anxiety, bursts of joy, and flow of love that are experienced are highly subjective and on the fringes of logical explanation. The quality of the interaction is both extremely personal and universal, in that many people feel pulled into the center of their being as well as feeling at one with all creation.

Above: A moment that defies description—Five-year-old Maggie, a child with leukemia, at the Dolphin Research Center.

From Jo Benton, Executive Director, Adirondack Mountain Club, Lake George, New York:

I think of the dolphins often and feel a link to them. Some of the feelings cannot be transcribed into words, perhaps because of the way they communicate. So many of our experiences with dolphins are in that domain beyond words. We receive something from them that we know intuitively and cannot verbalize.

Linda and Little Bit

Linda first visited the Dolphin Research Center in 1990 for the dolphin-human therapy program, a supervised encounter reserved for children and adults with all manner of disabilities. Although keenly aware of her environment and an avid swimmer, Linda had lost her eyesight five years earlier to juvenile diabetes.

Having been a professional nature photographer before losing her eyesight, Linda is still visually oriented and grasps layouts, images, colors, and scenes quite readily. Her other senses have become heightened, particularly her intuition.

Linda and her brother Michael interacted in the water with Little Bit (a dolphin definitely not named for her size, since she was over nine feet long). As she swam in the lagoon with her brother and Little Bit, Linda delighted in diving, bobbing, and swirling, to which the big lady dolphin responded by imitating her every move. She was amazed at how agile and loving Little Bit was and sensed that the dolphin was aware of her condition. Linda wrote of her encounter with Little Bit:

She would come up beside me and hover on my right side, offering to take me for a ride. It was a marvelous feeling being whooshed through the water at top speed, knowing I was being guided by a loving, sensitive, conscious being. As we returned to the dock, she stayed there with me and I sensed the tenderness with which she was observing me. Perhaps she noticed the problem with my eyes because at that point she became more protective and gentle in her moves. I have the wonderful memory of stroking her under her chin and kissing her on the snout, telling her, "You are just pure love."

For hours afterwards, I seemed to be floating. I could not attach my thoughts to anything else that made a difference in my life. Schedules and objectives that had seemed tremendously important before, evaporated into thin air. I was not concerned with details or personal objectives, rather, I had the feeling that everything around me was operating in perfect harmony. There was a divine synchronicity to all that was taking place. I felt happy doing nothing.

For days and weeks afterward, I could return to the feeling of the total experience whenever I chose to do so. Even though I am not able to see, I could just close my eyes, signifying the return to a calm and peaceful place and the joy would surface from deep within me...

There has been a feeling of love and freedom pervading my awareness. This is a new dimension of realization for me since the love in my life, in terms of relationships, had always had strings attached. In my own mind, I had associated experiencing love with living up to expectations. It seems that my experience of swimming with the dolphin liberated me from many of my limited concepts.

Living from the Heart

"Living from the Heart" is a program designed to help people suffering from stress-related and terminal illnesses. Since stress is believed to have an adverse effect on the immune system, stress-reduction can be an important factor in building the strength of the immune system. The Living from the Heart program combined workshops and therapy with time spent relating to the dolphins at the Dolphin Research Center. Whether or not being around dolphins improved their chances for a physical cure, people with serious illnesses relished the opportunity to relax in the warm Florida Keys sunshine, meditate to the sound of dolphins breathing, and absorb the energy of the dolphins. Program coordinator Kathi Rogers has been around dolphins enough to know that there is always something to be learned when you are open to the experience. Kathi tells us:

Nat was the handsomest dolphin of all. I fell in love with him right away. One day, early on, I went down on the floating dock in his lagoon. I told him that I didn't know how to communicate with dolphins—could he teach me? I sat down and waited. Nat swam around. He'd look at me on the way by. Nothing. I waited. He swam around some more. I waited. I started to feel foolish—to think I could hear what a dolphin had to say—or that he had something to say to me. Maybe it was possible, but nothing was happening here.

After waiting another long while, I said good-bye. As I stepped off the floating dock onto the boardwalk, I heard clearly in my mind, "Keep your heart open always." I sat down again, stunned. In spite of myself, I had heard him. When I let go—gave up—in that split second of open space he leaped into my heart and I could hear the words. Nat came around again. "Always?" I asked. That seemed pretty tough for us humans. Already I was questioning! Nat just swam by.

Twice more I heard him during that first week of Living from the Heart— "Accept without judgment," and, "Love without reason." Each time I heard what he had to say was when I gave up thinking it would happen. That seems to be how it is with dolphins.

Therapeutic Touch

Staff at the Dolphin Research Center schedule different kinds of sessions with the dolphins to ensure that the dolphins' days have variety and balance. In feeding sessions, the dolphins can just sit at the dock and receive their fish, although it's likely that they will swim back and forth, eating some, then showing off their favorite behaviors and generally cutting up. They don't need to do this to get fish, but they get so much enthusiastic positive reinforcement in the way of applause and attention from delighted volunteers, students, and staff, that it seems to be just more fun for them to have their meals this way. Training sessions are different. It's then that the dolphins are asked to focus and learn any of a number of behaviors on signal.

Play sessions are just that—no fish, no trainers' whistles, just games and the dolphins' favorite playthings. These sessions are a chance for the dolphins to interact on their own terms. A quieter session of this sort is based on the principles of therapeutic touch and provides an opportunity to experience the quality of the dolphin's energy and mood, to observe without expectation.

From Susie's journal, November 1993:

I'm sitting cross-legged on the floating dock in Rainbow and Sandy's pool, arms in the water up past my elbows, leaning over as far as possible without falling in, with Sandy's tail fluke between my hands. I can't see much of the rest of Sandy, because he's hanging head down in the water. The fluke itself is firm and smooth between my flat hands; my extended fingers touch that narrow juncture where the flukes join the perpendicular tail stock; it feels very soft where the tail stock starts to flare between my index and third fingers. Such a subtle thing, but the sensation is very firmly impressed on my memory.

Although Sandy is hanging straight down in the water from my hands, obviously I'm not holding him. For one thing, he must weigh around six hundred pounds. For another, he's very strong. To get into this delicate position, first Sandy cruises next to the dock. He loves back rubs; at least, he often positions himself for them. I run my hands lightly over his back, from behind the blowhole to his dorsal fin. As he moves forward, he slows, offering his tail, and I wrap my hands under the forward edges of his flukes as he stops and sinks. At first I am holding his tail, but as we both subtly adjust to the position, I can move my hands up so they are just pressing on the top and bottom of his tail, like hands folded in prayer, pointing down. I don't know how the dolphins do it, balance in the water like this—Sandy must be doing something, but remains motionless and seems completely relaxed. It's as though we are enveloped by the same energy field, flowing between us and around us.

Minutes go by, I have no idea how many in this timeless moment. The late afternoon sunlight filters through the mangroves and dances in the water. I sense a change in Sandy and remove my hands as he curves up to the surface to breathe. His breath is so soft and easy. Sometimes Sandy can be kind of squirrely and wired, with lots of explosive energy. I think these times, when we relate without fish and without expectations, are as nice for him as they are for us.

It took awhile for some of the dolphins to get the idea that we weren't asking them to do anything in particular. I think the dolphins absolutely love these sessions. It seems to be very relaxing for them. It can leave me feeling drugged. Maybe it has something to do with the theory that being around dolphins (relaxed dolphins, anyway) can bring your brain into an alpha state, alpha waves being the type of activity experienced in the trance-like state of meditation and deep relax-

ation. Sometimes I feel like I'm floating, really spacey, and have to ground myself before I drive home.

So many of the significant things that happen in our lives go beyond what we can adequately express in words. Whether falling in love, experiencing a delightful coincidence, being reunited with a friend, saying goodbye as death takes a loved one, or connecting with a dolphin—powerful experiences such as these don't need to be explained, only to be cherished.

Conclusion

BALANCE &
HARMONY

THE KEY TO a healthy and fulfilling life is balance, in the sense of being in balance with your environment, as well as balancing the various aspects of your nature. We are not all mind, all body, all heart, or all spirit. We are each an integrated whole, but neglecting any of our parts throws the organism out of balance. Flattening a wheel on one side does not make for smooth travel.

Mind

It is not enough to live by thought. With our highly developed brains, and all the demands our societies make on them, it's easy to get out of touch with the other parts of ourselves. The result can be an unhealthy, diseased body, stifled emotions, and a starved spirit.

Your mind is a tremendous gift, and it benefits from challenge and training. Living a conscious life means using your intellect to focus on and solve life's problems, using your analytical powers enhanced by your intuition. Your thoughts are powerful, and learning to foster positive thoughts can have a profound effect on what you do, how you feel, and who you are. We can use our minds to bring great good to our own species and to others on this planet. Life is more than human manifestation—our Earth vibrates with life in myriad forms. Each individual a musical note, each species a chord. How exciting and wonderful to be a part of that symphony.

Dolphins, with their complex society and well-developed brains, are in harmony with nature. We must keep our mental development from taking us so far out of touch with the Earth on which we rely for life that we destroy ourselves. We live on a finite planet with limited resources, which we are consuming as if there is no tomorrow. Separating ourselves from our habitat makes no sense.

From Susan Barco, Research Scientist, Virginia Marine Science Museum:
Man has always thought it was his place to control the environment and in doing so is systematically destroying it. A dolphin has the ultimate symmetry with the environment and works within its constraints.

Body

There is a wisdom that resides in the body, a wisdom we possess by virtue of being born into this world a physical being. People sometimes get away from the truth of their physical natures.

We can't all go back to the woods and live like other animals; we have to continue from where we are. But we are animals. We are born into the world as physical beings with blood and bones and flesh. We breath air, drink water; we eat and process food. We bring children into the world in the usual way—not so different from many other animals. We admire the majesty of nature and yet we distance ourselves from it, or society distances us from it.

To be healthy it is important to be in touch with your physical being, and this is something we can learn from the simple knowledge of animals, who eat when they are hungry, drink when they are thirsty, and mate when nature stirs their passions. Dolphins can help us bridge the gap, remember the benefits of our animal nature, while teaching us to use our well-developed brains for good, not ill.

Heart and Spirit

The following journal entry from Major's experiences in the Bahamas relates how he was abruptly called back to physical reality:

Yesterday afternoon I had an incredibly energizing, mesmerizing, peaceful, soul-searching, contemplative, spontaneous, unconditional love encounter in the water with ten spotted dolphins. The eye contact was indescribable.

I was so taken by the experience of the moment that it's lucky I'm alive to write about it. Not only did I forget to regularly surface for air and felt like I swallowed a few gallons of sea water, but I was so enraptured by the interaction that, at one point, I came up alongside one of the dolphins, both of us heading up for air, and conked my head on the bottom of the boat. I saw stars for a moment, almost blacking out, then still had to swim from under the boat and get to the surface for air!

As delightful as it may be to lose oneself in the euphoria of the moment, there are many situations in which it is useful to have your brain in gear! It is a question of balance.

Your body is the ship, your emotions are the sail, your mind is the rudder, and your spirit is the wind. If you are concerned with physical pleasure or fitness to the exclusion of developing your mind or nurturing your spirit, once again you run the risks of a life out of balance. And if your emotions rule your life—without the guidance of careful thought, the physical grounding brought by good care of your body, or the inspiration of the spirit—your journey through life is likely to be painful.

The benefits of nurturing your spirit will be seen in the increase of love, joy and kindness in your life. Our human communities are strengthened when the individuals within those communities live balanced lives. There is no limit to what you can achieve with a clear mind, a healthy body, balanced emotions, and a strong, loving spirit.

The wisdom of dolphins is that they are what they are. They are in touch with their inner nature. They can't describe to us what they are; they just are. In this simplicity is the most useful kind of wisdom.

From Susie's journal, July, 1998:

It's a hot, sultry morning—summer at the Virginia coast. I'm on a sixty-two-foot head boat, sitting up on the roof above the deck. Below on the deck are about seventy-five dolphin watchers, mostly tourists. Around us, swimming lazily about, are maybe fifty bottlenose dolphins.

We're drifting just a little ways off shore, and the dolphins are mostly between us and the beach. It amazes me how close in they go. A drowsy, contented mood settles over the scene. The dolphins may be fishing, but don't seem to me to be working very hard at anything. They are milling about, sometimes swimming over close to the boat, turning a mildly curious brown eye up our way, then meandering on. I see some sexual behavior over there; two dolphins, belly to belly, writhing and twisting, corkscrew up out of the water and go crashing over. Looks like there's a little knot of three or four involved in this dance, but it seems a fairly mellow and not overly serious business.

We saw dolphins as soon as we headed out of Rudee Inlet into the calm Atlantic this trip. The captain turned the big boat south, the direction the dolphins were traveling. Mornings, groupings of dolphins head out of the mouth of the Chesapeake Bay and travel south along the coast toward the North Carolina border; late afternoons we usually see them heading back north. They forage for the spot and croaker that inhabit the area, and also weakfish, sea trout, and menhaden, depending on the season.

Today, there were so many dolphins around, the tourists started to get used to them. It was too easy; no straining of the eyes to distinguish a possible dorsal fin. They were there, and we were among them. At first, of course, there is great excitement—the thrill of seeing the dolphins bow-riding, appearing just under the surface, speeding along with the bow wave; one rolls away, and another takes its place. I encourage the people to notice individual differences, a notched dorsal fin here, a scarred back there, and to distinguish between an irregularly shaped dorsal fin and the long strands of soft barnacles that hang off some of their dorsals like ragged flags.

It's great when we can see mothers and calves—it's early in the summer and some of those calves look pretty young. It's inexpressibly cute when the little round-eyed, snub-snouted black face of a newborn comes bobbing up beside its mother, catching a breath and poking back down in an awkward imitation of her smooth arcing motion. I tell the people as much as I think they can stand about dolphin behavior and basic physiology. They are so enchanted by the dolphins, they eat it all up. This is what I call educating the public.

That was about an hour ago. Now all of us—dolphins and humans—have settled into just hanging out. It really is ridiculously hot for 10:00 in the morning. The water shimmers. The dolphins splash gently. The people sit on the benches or hang over the rail, and watch. There is little talking—I can't believe a group this size is this quiet. A young couple is snuggling on a bench facing out toward the gentle orgy going on, and I know they feel that energy. We couldn't be more mellow. We are under the dolphins' spell.

Epilogue # TRANSFORMATION
GIVING SOMETHING BACK

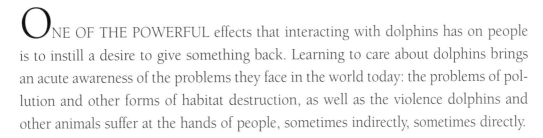

ONE OF THE POWERFUL effects that interacting with dolphins has on people is to instill a desire to give something back. Learning to care about dolphins brings an acute awareness of the problems they face in the world today: the problems of pollution and other forms of habitat destruction, as well as the violence dolphins and other animals suffer at the hands of people, sometimes indirectly, sometimes directly.

From Nicole Mader, Wild Dolphin Project, Jupiter, Florida:

Unfortunately, when I think of dolphins, sadness almost instantly comes to mind. It sounds so morbid, but the negative impact of humans upon this planet is mind-boggling. I wish the dolphins were able to kick our butts in shape and teach us how to live together without destroying their environment and each other.

Maybe they can. It's funny how this dolphin connection stuff works. Diane Ross, an actress and model from California, was visiting her sister in Hollywood, Florida. One day, on a lark, since they had never been to the Florida Keys, the two of them decided to drive to Key West. They made it as far as Duck Key, about halfway down the 129-mile-long chain of Keys, and were so tired they pulled into Hawk's Cay Resort & Marina to find a room for the night. Unbeknownst to them, Hawk's Cay had a dolphin facility right there at the resort.

Diane was mesmerized by the dolphins and watched them most of the night from the deck of the resort as they peacefully swam about their lagoons, exhaling those misty breaths of air. She had never seen dolphins up close and didn't know the first thing about them. Someone at the resort suggested that they check out the Dolphin Research Center, only a few miles down the road.

The next day, they visited DRC, took the public tour, and also learned about DRC's week-long Dolphinlab program. Diane attended Dolphinlab some time later, and voraciously absorbed everything they offered. She heard about Denise Herzing's Wild Dolphin Project in the Bahamas from one of the Dolphinlab instructors, and went out with Denise the following summer. After many years of learning and dedicated volunteer work, Diane is now the Board President of the Wild Dolphin

Project—all this resulted from being tired of driving and pulling into Hawk's Cay on the way to Key West! Diane now has this to say about the impact of dolphins on her life, and on others she has observed:

> *Throughout my years of working with the Wild Dolphin Project, I have been incredibly fortunate to have had many phenomenal encounters both interacting with and observing wild dolphins. I have also felt great joy as others try to describe their personal reactions after being in the water with such magnificent beings.*
>
> *I have little doubt that all will agree with me when I conclude that something much bigger has transcended us in these moments. We have communicated with an alien species. And maybe, just maybe, that is enough.*

Many organizations played a role in educating Diane about marine mammals and the problems they encounter in the wild. There are barely enough facilities to handle the interest the public expresses. Surely the millions of people who visit these facilities each year could not afford to, nor should they ever attempt to, go out in boats to see dolphins in the wild—that would be devastating to wild populations. Your intentions may be benign, but what if wild dolphins find themselves visited each year by thousands or millions of people, all with benign intentions? It's a question being pondered by those familiar with wild pods, who view the increased public interest in wild dolphins with some alarm. This is why responsible programs are licensed and respect the limitations imposed by the Marine Mammal Protection Act.

Maintaining a balance is the key. Many learn about and study marine mammals at colleges and universities and the various public facilities around the world; others go out on the waters and study them in their natural habitats. Scientific research can work hand-in-hand with public education to promote the survival of marine mammals everywhere.

Dolphins heighten our awareness and provide the emotional link that drives people to care about the marine environment. It's harder to get people excited about saving a species of mussel they've never heard of, even though the endangered mussel may in fact provide an early warning of serious problems that can affect us all. Dolphins have become ambassadors for life in the ocean.

A deep-sea fishing boat was headed back to the marina after a fruitless half-day on the beautiful waters of the Florida Keys. While still a few miles out to sea, the anglers noticed a fairly large object churning up the water nearby. Upon investigating, they were shocked to find an adult dolphin completely entangled in a combination of discarded wire, netting, and rope. Apparently its efforts to free itself had only made matters worse.

The captain edged the boat as close to the dolphin as possible, while the first mate used a pole with a hook on the end to latch on to the netting and pull the dolphin alongside. The animal appeared to be very weak and had gashes and scrapes all over its body. Maybe sensing a desire on the part of the anglers to help, or maybe just because of exhaustion, the dolphin remained calm for the next forty-five minutes while the debris was untangled and cut loose. One of the guests aboard had a video camera and filmed the entire event. When the final piece of netting was removed, the dolphin swam slowly away, repeatedly looking back at the boat in a manner which to the anglers seemed to mean, "Thank you!"

The video was given to a local television station in Key West and was shown repeatedly for months as the station's viewers kept requesting it. The boat captain, and many captains of other crafts in the area, continue to tell of seeing this dolphin on their way in and out for deep-sea trips. Although it is not unusual for dolphins to come up alongside fishing boats and ride in their bow wake, they first recognized this particular dolphin from the easily identifiable gashes and scrapes. The captains watched it get healthier week after week as the cuts healed. But what they found most exciting was the manner in which this dolphin would approach their boats, pop up and down out of the water, or come barreling straight out and spin or flop onto the water's surface making a huge splash. To the captains, this dolphin was continually expressing its joy and thanks for being rescued.

People's lives are transformed by their fascination with dolphins, as in the case of Carol Chass, an enthusiastic wife and mother turned volunteer and educator:

> *I still today have a hard time explaining the special connection I feel with dolphins, except it's like how we feel the wind, and although you can't see it, you know it's there. Like God and love, I know it's there and just can't explain it!*

In 1985, my husband John and I were having breakfast with our two sons, when I overheard a customer telling the waitress how he had just returned from vacation. He went on to say that he had been at a facility and swum with dolphins. WOW!!! I had never realized that was possible. Poor John, for the next five years, every time we planned our family vacation, I would say, "I want to go wherever I can swim with the dolphins," even though I'm a non-swimmer.

After considerable letter writing by John to every Chamber of Commerce in the state of Florida, in search of his wife's dream, the answer arrived from Marathon, Florida, telling us about the Dolphin Research Center. By this time, our two sons were grown and not interested in going on vacation with mom and dad. So off we went, just John and I.

On February 18, 1990, we swam with two "angels of the sea"—Little Bit and her daughter Tursi. With the exception of finding my wonderful husband and having two great sons, I have never had anything else affect me the way this dolphin encounter did. The dolphins took a shy, introverted lady and changed her life completely from that day forward. There is a love, spirit, and soul connection still between us that I cannot put into appropriate words. When I am with them, I don't even notice if anyone else is there.

I returned home and wrote everyone I knew, and didn't know, about the horror of the dolphins being killed by the tuna industry. I also wanted to help spread the word about how we all need to get involved in the care of "Our Planet–Our Home."

I returned to the DRC and took every educational program they had to offer. My biggest problem was figuring out how to get the attention of strangers to help me spread the word. I came up with attracting attention by wearing dolphin shirts, accessories, and a lot of dolphin jewelry! Now the people in Kansas City, or wherever I travel, have nicknamed me "The Dolphin Lady" They don't remember my name—just the wearing of the dolphins.

I volunteer at the DRC at least three times a year. Each visit is a learning and work experience. Back at home I work on the Dolphin Outreach Program in the local schools. This is a free educational program to help spread the word about dolphins and what we can do to make their home and ours a better place.

If anyone had told me ten years ago that I would be out doing public speaking, I would have laughed and said, "Sorry, that's not for me, excuse me while I hide." However, the love, communication, and connection with the dolphins has changed that for me forever. Now my only wish is to somehow return that love to them by being one of the "human voices" trying to preserve the quality of their ocean home.

Beth Stark, Animal Enrichment Director for the Toledo, Ohio, Zoo and a former dolphin trainer, sums it up beautifully:

I remember the first day I worked with dolphins as if it was yesterday. I often reflect on that day—the smile on my face and the incredible joy in my heart—and draw upon that feeling when I'm down, lonely, or just contemplative. As my work and my career progressed, I discovered the different personalities of each dolphin and began to appreciate this species even more, not in a mystical sense, but as living, breathing creatures who, by their presence in our world, and our presence in theirs, have affected so many people in many positive ways. In a world of so much destruction, hurt, and heartbreak, dolphins, for whatever reason, have positively influenced people to think about our impact on the fragile environment and take action to conserve it for future generations of all species to inhabit.

May our love for dolphins inspire us to seek out true things about them that will be more mutually beneficial than anything our fantasies have told us.

RESOURCES

BOOKS

The Audubon Society Field Guide to North American Fishes, Whales & Dolphins. Alfred A. Knopf, 1988.

Barnes, Robert, *The Blue Dolphin.* H. J. Kramer, Inc., 1994.

Burgess, Robert F., *Secret Languages of the Sea.* Dodd, Mead & Co., 1988.

Catton, Chris, *Dolphins.* St. Martin's Press, 1995.

Cochran, Amanda, and Karena Callen, *Dolphins and Their Power to Heal.* Bloomsbury Publishing, London, 1992.

Doak, Wade, *Encounters with Whales & Dolphins.* Hodder & Stoughton, Auckland, Australia, 1981.

Dobbs, Horace, *Follow a Wild Dolphin.* Souvenir Press, London, 1977.

_____, *Tale of Two Dolphins.* Jonathan Cape Ltd., London, 1987.

Earle, Sylvia A., *Sea Change, A Message of the Oceans.* Fawcett Books, 1996.

_____, *Dive: My Adventures in the Deep Frontier.* National Geographic Society, 1999.

_____, *Wild Ocean, America's Parks Under the Sea.* National Geographic Society, 1999.

Goldman, Daniel, *Emotional Intelligence.* Bantam Books, 1995.

Griffin, Donald, *Animal Minds.* Univ. of Chicago Press, 1992.

_____, *The Question of Animal Awareness.* Rockefeller Univ. Press, 1976.

Grover, Wayne, *Dolphin Adventure, A True Story.* William Morrow & Co., 1990.

Herman, L. M., Ed., *Cetacean Behavior, Mechanisms and Function.* John Wiley & Sons, 1980.

Horton, Casey, *Dolphins.* Cavendish, Marshall Corp., 1995.

Howard, Carol, *Dolphin Chronicles.* Bantam, 1995.

Katz, Welwyn Wilton, *Whale-singer.* McElderry Books, 1990.

Leatherwood, S., and R. R. Reeves, *The Bottlenose Dolphin.* Academic Press, 1990.

Lilly, John, *Communication Between Man and Dolphin.* Julian Press, 1978.

_____, *Mind of a Dolphin.* Doubleday, 1967.

Lynch, Dudley, and Kordis, Paul, *Strategy of the Dolphin.* Fawcett-Columbine, 1988.

Masson, Jeffrey, and Susan McCarthy, *When Elephants Weep, The Emotional Lives of Animals*. Delacorte Press, 1995.

McKenna, Virginia, *Into the Blue*. Aquarian Press, London, 1992.

Miller, Lana, *Call of the Dolphins*. Rainbow Bridge Publishing, 1989.

Nakamura, Tsuneo, and Randall Wells (Intro), *Dolphins*. Chronicle Books, 1997.

Nielsen, Ashleea, *Dolphin Tribe*. Dancing Dolphin Press, 1994.

Norris, Kenneth S., *The Porpoise Watcher*. W. W. Norton & Co., Inc., 1974.

——————————, *Dolphin Days, The Life and Times of Spinner Dolphins*. W. W. Norton & Co., Inc., 1991.

—————————— with Bernd and Melany Wursig, *The Hawaiian Spinner Dolphin*. Univ. of California Press, 1994.

Oden, ViAnn, *Dialogue with a Dolphin*. Anvipa Press, 1991.

Pryor, Karen, and Kenneth S. Norris (eds.), *Dolphin Societies, Discoveries and Puzzles*. Univ. of California Press, 1991.

Quayle, Louise, *Dolphins and Porpoises*. Gallery Books, 1988.

Ridgway, Sam, *The Dolphin Doctor*. Ballantine Books, 1988.

Ridgway, S. H., and R. Harrison (eds.), *Handbook of Marine Mammals, Vol. 6, the Second Book of Dolphins and Porpoises*. Academic Press, 1999.

Scanlan, Phillip M., and Steven Ott (Intro), *The Dolphins Are Back*. Productivity Press Inc., 1998.

Schusterman, Ronald J., Jeanette A. Thomas and Forrest G. Wood (eds.). *Dolphin Cognition and Behavior, A Comparative Approach*. Lawrence Eribaum Associates, 1986.

Shane, Susan, *The Bottlenose Dolphin in the Wild*. Hatcher Trade Press, 1988.

Thorne-Miller, Boyce, and Sylvia A. Earle (Forward), *The Living Ocean, Understanding and Protecting Marine Biodiversity*. Island Press, 1998.

Varawa, Joana McIntyre, *The Delicate Art of Whale Watching*. Sierra Club Books, 1991.

White, Thomas, *Discovering Philosophy*. Prentice Hall, 1989.

Williams, Heathcote, *Falling for a Dolphin*. Jonathan Cape Ltd., London, 1988.

Wilson, Ben, *Dolphins of the World*. Voyageur Press, Inc., 1998.

YOUNG PEOPLE'S BOOKS

Buffett, Jimmy, and Savannah Jane Buffett, *The Jolly Mon*. Harcourt Brace & Co., 1988.

Burke, Terrill Miles, *Dolphin Magic* series. Alpha-Dolphin Press, Book One 1992, Book Two 1993.

Cerullo, Mary M., *Dolphins: What They Can Teach Us*. Dutton Children's Books, 1999.

Cummings, Jim, *A Friend in the Water*. Healing Earth Publications, 1988.

Earle, Sylvia, *Hello, Fish! Visiting the Coral Reef*. National Geographic Society, 1999.

Hatherly, Janelle, and Delia Nicholls, *Dolphins and Porpoises*. Facts On File, Inc., 1994.

Rinard, Judith E., *Dolphins, Our Friends in the Sea*. National Geographic Society, 1986.

Stoops, Erik D., Jeffrey L. Martin and Debbie Lynne Stone, *Dolphins*. Sterling Publ. Co., 1998.

TRIPS AND PROGRAMS

Dolphin Connection, Hawks Cay Resort & Marina, MM# 61, Duck Key, Marathon, FL 33050. Phone: 305-289-9975.
Website: www.dolphinconnection.com.

Dolphin Research Center, P.O. Box 522875, Marathon Shores, FL 33052-2875.
Phone: 305-289-1121; Fax: 305-743-7627.
Email: drc@reefnet.com.
Website: www.dolphins.org.

Dolphin Watch, Capt. Ron Canning, Key West, FL 33040. Phone: 305-294-6306.
Email: dolwatch@aol.com.
Website: www.dolphinwatchusa.com.

The Dream Team, Capt. Wayne "Scott" Smith, P. O. Box 12714, Lake Park, FL 33403-2714.
Phone: 888-277-8181; Fax: 561-840-7746.
Website: www.dolphindreamteam.com.

Earthwatch, 680 Mt. Auburn St., P. O. Box 9104, Watertown, MA 02272,
Phone: 800-776-0188.
Email: info@earthwatch.org.
Website: www.earthwatch.org.

Hyatt Regency Waikoloa, HC02 Box 5500, Waikoloa, HI 96743. Phone: 808-885-1234.

Institute of Marine Sciences, Roatan, Bay Island, Honduras, Central America.
Phone: 011 504 451327.

Oceanic Society Expeditions, Fort Mason Center, Building E, Suite E240, San Francisco, CA 94123. Phone: 415-441-1106.

Theater of the Sea, 84721 Overseas Highway, Islamorada, FL 33036. Phone: 305-664-2431. Email: info@theaterofthesea.com. Website: www.theaterofthesea.com.

UNEXSO, P.O. Box 5608, Ft. Lauderdale, FL 33310. Phone: 800-992-DIVE or 305-359-2730. Bahamas phone number: 809-373-1244. Email: info@unexso.com. Website: www.unexso.com.

Wild Dolphin Project, 21 Hepburn Ave., Suite 20, Jupiter, FL 33458 (Denise Herzing). Phone: 407-575-5660. Email: wdp@igc.org. Website: www.wwwa.com/dolphin.

Organizations

American Cetacean Society, P.O. Box 1391, San Pedro, CA 90733-1391. Phone: 310-548-6279. Email: acs@pobox.com. Website: www.acsonline.org.

American Oceans Campaign, 725 Arizona Ave., Suite 102, Santa Monica, CA 90401. Phone: 310-576-6162. Email: aoc@earthlink.net. Website: www.americanoceans.org.

Center for Cetacean Research and Conservation, 800 Mere Point Road, Brunswick, ME 04011. Phone: 207-729-1543. Email: blowholes@ime.net.

Center for Marine Conservation, 1725 DeSales Street NW, Washington, DC 20036. Website: www.cmc-ocean.org.

Cetacean Research Unit, P.O. Box 159, Gloucester, MA 01931-0159

College of the Atlantic (Marine Mammal Laboratory), 105 Eden St., Bar Harbor, ME 04609. Phone: 207-288-5015. Website: www.coa.edu.

Dolphin Connection, Hawks Cay Resort & Marina, MM# 61, Duck Key, Marathon, FL 33050. Phone: 305-289-9975. Website: www.dolphinconnection.com.

Dolphin Ecology Project, P.O. Box 1142, Key Largo, FL 33070. Phone: 305-852-0649. Email: DolphinEco@aol.com.

Dolphin Institute, The, 420 Ward Avenue, Suite 220, Honolulu, HI 96814 (Kewalo Basin Marine Mammal Laboratory). Website: www.dolphin-institute.org.

Dolphin Research Center, P. O. Box 522875, Marathon Shores, FL 33050-2875. Phone: 305-289-1121. Email: drc@reefnet.com. Website: www.dolphins.org.

Dolphin Society, P.O. Box 2052, Clovelly, NSW 2031, Australia. Email: dolphins@dolphinsoc.org. Website: www.eisa.net.au/~dolphins.

Earthtrust, 25 Kaneohe Bay Dr., Suite 205, Kailua, HI 96734. Phone: 808-254-2866. Email: et@lava.net. Website: www.earthtrust.org.

International Cetacean Education Research Centre, P.O. Box 110, Nambucca, New South Wales, Australia 2448.

International Cetacean Education Research Centre (ICERC) Japan, 4A, 5-3-3 Shirogenedai, Minato-Ku, Tokyo 108, Japan.

International Dolphin Watch, Parklands, North Ferriby, Humberside HU14 3ET, England.

International Marine Animal Trainer's Association (IMATA). Website: www.imata.org.

Kahua Hawaiian Institute, P.O. Box 1747, Makawao, HI 96768.

Marine Mammal Stranding Center, P.O. Box 773, Brigantine, NJ 08203.

Mote Marine Laboratory, 1600 Ken Thompson Parkway, Sarasota FL 34236. Phone: 941-388-4441. Website: www.mote.org.

Nature Conservancy, The, 4245 North Fairfax Drive, Suite 100, Arlington, VA 22203. Web Site: www.tnc.org.

Northeast Marine Animal Lifeline, P.O. Box 453, Biddeford, ME 04005. Phone: 207-773-7377. Email: nmal@ime.net. Website: http://lincoln.midcoast.com/~nemal.

Ocean Alliance/Whale Conservation Institute, 191 Weston Road, Lincoln, MA 01733. Phone: 781-259-0423, 800-96WHALE. Email: question@oceanalliance.org. Website: www.oceanalliance.org.

Oceania Project, P.O. Box 646, Byron Bay, Australia NSW 2481.

Pacific Whale Foundation, 101 N. Kihei Rd., Kihei, Maui, HI 96753.

Port Phillip Bay Dolphin Research Project, P.O. Box 774, Rye, Victoria 3941, Australia.

Scripps Institution of Oceanography, University of California, San Diego, 8602 La Jolla Shores Drive, La Jolla, CA 92037. Website: http://sio.ucsd.edu.

Sea Watch Foundation, 7 Andrews Lane, Southwater, West Sussex, RH13 7DY, England. Website: http://ourworld.compuserve.com.

Society of Marine Mammalogy, Washington Cooperative Fish and Wildlife Research Unit, School of Fisheries, Box 357980, University of Washington, Seattle, WA 98195. Publishes quarterly journal, "Marine Mammal Science." Website: http://pegasus.cc.ucf.edu.

Virginia Institute of Marine Science (College of William & Mary), P.O. Box 1346, Gloucester Point, VA 23062. Website: www.vims.edu.

Virginia Marine Science Museum, 717 General Booth Boulevard, Virginia Beach, VA 23451, Phone: 757-425-3474. Website: www.va-beach.com/va-marine-science-museum.

Whale Conservation Institute/Ocean Alliance, 191 Weston Road, Lincoln, MA 01733, Phone: 781-259-0423, 800-96WHALE. Email: question@oceanalliance.org. Website: www.oceanalliance.org.

Woods Hole Oceanographic Institution, Woods Hole, MA 02543-1539, 508-457-2000. Website: www.whoi.edu.

World Wildlife Fund, 1250 Twenty-Fourth Street NW, Washington, DC 20037. Website: www.worldwildlife.org

WEB SITES

www.marine-ed.org An on-line ocean education clearinghouse developed by VIMS (Virginia Institute of Marine Science) in conjunction with NMEA (National Marine Educators Association), the national network of Sea Grant educators, and NOPP (National Ocean Partnership Program).

whale.wheelock.edu/ See "WhaleNet," an inter-active education project focusing on whales and marine research, sponsored by Wheelock College in Boston, Massachusetts, with support from the National Science Foundation.

sustainableseas.noaa.gov The Sustainable Seas Expeditions aim to study the ocean with unprecedented scientific rigor. The project focuses on the twelve marine sanctuaries designated and protected by the United States government.

www.sanctuaries.nos.noaa.gov The prime vehicle for communicating information about the management programs, scientific activities, news and events for our nation's marine sanctuaries.

www.nmfs.gov/prot_res/prot_res.html The National Marine Fisheries Service, Office of Protected Resources. All cetacean species are protected by the Marine Mammal Protection Act of 1972. Learn about the seven species of cetaceans in U.S. waters that are protected under the Endangered Species Act.

pegasus.cc.ucf.edu/~smm/ The site for the Society for Marine Mammalogy (which has lots of links). The Society also publishes the quarterly journal, "Marine Mammal Science."

INDEX

63-72; curiosity, 63-72; death, 18-19, 125-133; evolution, 75; feeding strategies, 23, 24-25, 68-71, 101-102; games, 110-11; helping behaviors, 26-27, 103-104, 106; humor, 33, 35-36, 112-114; hunting, 24, See also dolphins, feeding strategies; imitation, 65-66; individuality, 2, 31-37; intelligence, x, 41-47; innovation , 64-65; language,3-5; learning, 43-45; male, 14-15, 16-17; mothering, 14, 19-20, 33-34, 34-35, 90, 98-102, 130; movement, 75-81; nursing, 98-100, 101; painting, 31-32, 35; physiology, 76-77, 90, 99; pods, 23-24, 26-27; relationships, 1, 13-21; Risso's, 16; river, xi; rough-toothed, 16; senses, 83-88; sexual behavior, 79, 85-86; skin, 84; sleep, 91; society, 1-2, 13-19, 101-102; sounds, 5-7; spinner, 24, 77; spotted, xii, xx, 16, 78, 88, 130; threats, 26, 130-131; training, 49-61; vocal structures, 6-7

"Dolphin Tales" (Smith), 139

E

echolocation, 7-8, 24, 67, 79, 84

Engleby, Laura Urian, 18-19, 35-36

Erb, Linda, 28, 35, 132

F

false killer whales, 136-137

Fink, Jane, 104-105

fishermen, 24-25

Florida Keys National Marine Sanctuary, 103

H

Hali (dolphin), 138, 139

Hampp, Joy, xi

Haverford College, 45

Herman, Louis, 43

hippopotamus, 75

human: communication, 9-12; cooperation, 29-30; evolution, xvi-xvii; inner nature, 36-37; mind, 47-48; relationships, 20-21; society, 29-30

J

Jakush, Greg, 58-59

K

Kewalo Basin Marine Mammal Laboratory, 43

Kibby (dolphin),16-17, 31, 32, 49, 59, 66

L

Lerner, Heidi, 4

ABOUT THE AUTHORS

Laura Engleby

Susan Yoder specializes as a writer and educator in the appreciation and conservation of natural resources. As an interpreter and outreach instructor for the Virginia Marine Science Museum, she led dolphin-watch boat trips and brought interactive programs to schools and organizations throughout the mid-Atlantic region. She worked as an educator and dolphin handler at the Dolphin Research Center on Grassy Key, Florida.

Major Benton is a Conservation Officer for the Virginia State Parks. He managed the Chicago Zoological Society's Dolphin Connection program at Hawk's Cay on Duck Key, Florida, and writes environmental, human interest, and other non-fiction articles from travels, research, and experiences.

Susan Yoder and Major Benton are sponsors of a beautiful, full-color, 18 x 20-inch poster of nineteen-year-old dolphin "Tursi" spinning out of the water in a circle of spray and light. Photographed by Mary Ann Little at the Dolphin Research Center. Posters sell for $16.90 (includes shipping and handling) and benefit the Dolphin Research Center.

Yoder and Benton also publish *MajorSigns,* a quarterly journal with stories of inspiration, humor and insight to encourage creativity and networking. Subscriptions are $10 per year, $3 for a sample issue.

For more information or to order the "Tursi" poster or the *MajorSigns* journal, send an e-mail to majorsigns@aol.com

THE DOLPHIN DREAM TEAM
SPEND A WEEK ABOARD
THE DREAM TOO

Join Capt. Wayne "Scott" Smith and the Dolphin Dream Team for a week-long excursion on their sixty-five-foot charter/research vessel to the beautiful blue waters of the Bahamas. A once-in-a-lifetime experience awaits you among the wild dolphins of the Little Bahama Bank with the guidance of those who know and love them. Capt. Smith spends over thirty-five weeks per year in the Bahamas with the dolphins.

THIS COUPON IS REDEEMABLE FOR A 10 PERCENT DISCOUNT
OFF THE PRICE OF YOUR EXCURSION*

Phone 888-277-8181 to take advantage of this offer, or write to:

The Dream Team, Inc.

P.O. Box 12714, Lake Park, FL 33404-2714

(*subject to availability, especially during peak seasons)

Check out the Dolphin Dream Team website at www.dolphindreamteam.com or send e-mail to dream2@gate.net for more information.

The Dolphin Dream Team is an organization dedicated to documenting the lives and behaviors of Atlantic spotted dolphins. Knowing the dolphins and their habits will help maintain a safe environment for future generations to enjoy.

DOLPHIN RESEARCH CENTER, GRASSY KEY, FLORIDA

Dolphin Research Center is a not-for-profit education and research facility, home to a colony of about fifteen bottlenose dolphins in a natural marine environment on the Gulf of Mexico. Many of the dolphins were born there, others came from other facilities to retire, and a few old-timers came from the wild, collected by other management many years ago.

The Dolphin Research Center offers programs for visitors to its educational and research facility, including daily tours, views behind the scenes during dolphin training sessions, workshops, structured swims, internships volunteer programs, and dolphin adoption programs.

WITH THIS COUPON, RECEIVE A FREE TWO-MONTH ASSOCIATE MEMBERSHIP TO DOLPHIN RESEARCH CENTER THAT INCLUDES THEIR NEWSLETTER AND INFORMATION ON THEIR ADOPT-A-DOLPHIN PROGRAM.

Name _____

Address _____

_____

Phone _____ Email Address _____

Mail coupon to:

Dolphin Research Center, Attention: Membership Coordinator
P.O. Box 522875, Marathon Shores, FL 33052-2875

For information on their programs, please visit the Dolphin Research Center website at www.dolphins.org. Or if you prefer, call (305) 289-1121 or email: drc@dolphins.org .

The Dolphin Research Center receives no government funding. Your membership donation helps them provide the best of care for the dolphins and continue to offer educational programs to the public.